Pasta

MURDOCH BOOKS

Pasta

Basics to Brilliance
Techniques, Tips and Trusted Recipes

• MASTERING THE BASICS •

Contents

Introduction

Spaghetti Bolognese, Pasta Puttanesca and Lasagne. Is there anything that conjures up the beautiful flavours of Italy more evocatively than these classic pasta dishes? While the Ancient Greeks or Etruscans were the first to cook and eat pasta more than 7000 years ago, it was the Italians who well and truly mastered the art and who have given us these classic pasta dishes.

Thanks to the range of dishes available, their versatility and plain deliciousness, pasta is as popular now as it ever has been. With more than 70 approachable yet inspirational recipes for both everyday eating and entertaining, together with clear step-by-step instructions, *Mastering the Basics: Pasta* will become your everyday guide to these indispensable staples. The techniques explained in the Basics chapter, such as making and cooking the perfect pasta, support the recipes and will build your skills so you have the confidence needed to master any pasta. Enjoy!

Pasta Basics

Types of pasta

Dried pasta

Dried pasta is one of the main staples of the modern pantry. It's always on hand, quick and easy to prepare, and nutritious. Dried pasta is also sturdier than fresh and pairs with more flavour options than delicate-tasting fresh pasta.

Dried pasta is the one to choose for hearty tomato sauces. It has also traditionally been used to hold richer, oil-based sauces that contain olives, anchovies, meat or seafood, as it has a firmer, denser texture than fresh pasta when cooked. Flavours such as spinach and tomato may also be added to dried pasta. When shopping, it is worth spending a little extra money when buying dried pasta and getting a good-quality brand — inferior brands can have a disappointing texture.

Dried pasta is made with flour, water and sometimes eggs. Dried pasta made with 100 per cent durum wheat flour (durum wheat is a variety with a higher gluten content) is considered to be of superior quality. Pasta made with wholemeal flour is darker and nuttier in flavour. Dried pastas can also be made with flour ground from other cereals, such as corn, buckwheat, rice and soya beans.

There are many shapes and sizes and a lot of information can be gleaned from the name of a type of pasta. A name ending in -ricce means the pasta has a wavy edge; rigate means ridged; and lisce means smooth surfaced. Some names are visual descriptions of the shape: orecchiette are little ears; eliche (a type of spiral pasta) are propellers; ditali (small short tubes) are thimbles; conchiglie are shells; linguine are little tongues; while vermicelli are little worms.

giant fusilli

fettuccine

cannelloni

vermicelli

tagliatelle

orecchiette

Dried pasta keeps its flavour if stored airtight for up to two years. Dried egg pasta and wholemeal pasta don't last as long — generally only a few months, but check the packet.

Dried long pasta can partner well with smooth tomato, creamy or oily sauces. Some of the wider long pastas can hold meat sauces too, as there is room for the sauce to nestle and cling to the pasta. Types include spaghetti, spaghettini, angel hair, linguine, fettuccine, bucatini, pappardelle and reginette.

Dried shapes for baking are perfect for meat and vegetable pasta dishes — it's convenient to use dried pasta for these dishes as you can keep various types on hand at all times.

Some recipes call for them to be blanched before filling or layering. Types include lasagne sheets, cannelloni, conchiglioni and ziti.

Dried large shapes are great for chunky sauces as the dips and curves give the sauce something to cling to. Types include conchiglie, penne, rigatoni, pipe rigate, fusilli, farfalle, orecchiette, rotelle and casarecci.

Dried small shapes are traditionally used with a simple sauce or as part of a soup. Children generally love small pasta shapes too. Types include macaroni, cavatelle, anelli, ditalini, stellini and risoni (also known as orzo).

cortecce

maccheroni al ferretto

macaroni

conchiglioni

penne

linguine

ditalini lisci

risoni

Fresh pasta

The only thing more rewarding than making your own pasta is eating it. There's a vast array of good-quality fresh pasta distributed directly from artisan pasta makers and often available at speciality delicatessens. Supermarkets also stock some fresh pasta products.

Once cooked, fresh pasta has a softer texture than dried pasta. This allows it to better absorb the flavours of the sauce it's served with. Fresh pasta can be the perfect foil for both rich creamy sauces and delicate seafood sauces. Ready-made fresh pasta is more expensive than dried, but, made by artisan producers, it is far superior to the entry-level supermarket brands. Buy the best you can afford.

Fresh pasta is generally made with flour, eggs and sometimes a little olive oil or water. The dough can also be flavoured with spinach, tomato, squid ink, saffron or herbs.

The best flour to use is 100 per cent durum wheat flour that is very finely milled and classified '00'. Organic eggs really make a difference too. It is also possible to replace some of the flour with wholemeal (whole grain) or buckwheat flour. Eggless pasta (noodles) can be made using regular flour and is suitable for rich sauces such as ragù. Regular flour can be replaced with rice flour, soy or mung bean starch and even potato starch to make a variety of noodles.

Fresh filled pasta has a long history, with every region in Italy having its own varieties with unique fillings and shapes. Cappelletti are formed by filling a round of pasta and intricately folding it to form 'little hats', while tortellini are shaped into 'courtesans' navels' — both types are originally from Emilia. Agnolotti, from Piedmonte, are rumoured to be named after their maker. Ravioli are from Liguria; the name comes from the verb 'to wrap'.

(tomato) pappardelle

spaghetti

lasagne sheets

fettuccine

Freshly rolled pasta can be dried and stored for up to one week (see page 13). If storing bought fresh pasta, check the packet for storage instructions. Many rolled and cut fresh pastas can be stored in the refrigerator, and filled pastas are often sold frozen.

Sheets and cut fresh pasta Cut pastas of various widths have different uses — sheets are used to make lasagne or rotolo (filled pasta rolls) or even modern open ravioli dishes. Long, thin pasta can suit tomato, seafood (such as crab) or light vegetable sauces. Thick cuts of pasta can support chunks of meat or even pieces of seafood. Remember that the simplest sauce will allow the pasta to be the hero of the dish. Types include angel hair, spaghettini, linguine, spaghetti, tagliatelle, fettuccine and pappardelle.

Filled fresh pasta You can buy it ready made or make your own (see pages 14–15) — there are many possibilities for fillings incorporating cheese, vegetables, meat and seafood. With filled pasta, it can be worth remembering that the pasta can be flavoured too, adding another dimension to the dish before you even add a sauce. Types include square ravioli (small and large), round ravioli, agnolotti, tortellini and cappelletti.

Gnocchi Really good gnocchi is made primarily with potato bound with a small amount of flour. It's generally served with a simple sauce, so that when eating you appreciate the light texture of the gnocchi. Ready-made fresh and frozen types are both readily available.

gnocchi

large ravioli

giant tortellini

ravioli made with spinach pasta

large oval ravioli

Pasta-making equipment

How much equipment you need — or want — to buy will depend on how often you intend to make your own pasta.

Basic equipment

Many of the following items are already standard in most kitchens. Even pasta machines need not be expensive; kitchenware chains often have reasonably priced models.

Hand-cranked pasta machines are good for the novice or occasional pasta maker. Look for a quality machine made of plated steel that has good gears and a sturdy handle. They are compact to store and attach to a work surface with a clamp.

Cutting attachments for pasta machines come in various types. The basic attachment cuts fettuccine or taglierini and generally comes with the machine. Other cutting attachments are available for pappardelle, linguine and capellini.

Deep saucepans allow pasta to move about freely as it cooks, which helps prevent it from sticking together. A pan about 24 cm (10 inches) in diameter, with a minimum capacity of about 8 litres (280 fl oz) is ideal. With a pan of this diameter, the whole base of the pan is close to the element or gas burner on a domestic cooktop, which means that the water will return to the boil quickly once you add the pasta.

Large, wide and deep frying or sauté pans with tight-fitting lids enable you to make the sauce, then have enough room in the pan to toss the drained pasta in the sauce.

Food processors can be used to bring the dough together. You will then need to knead the dough by hand.

Rolling pins are used for rolling out the dough before feeding it through the rollers of the pasta machine. A wooden one is best.

Colanders are used for draining pasta. Make sure the holes are not too big, otherwise you will lose fine pastas (such as angel hair) down the sink.

Broom handles or other round wooden poles are used for hanging pasta to dry. You could also use a thickish dowel.

Pastry brushes are used for brushing egg wash onto pasta when making filled pasta. It's a good idea to have a separate pastry brush that you keep dry and which is used solely to brush clean the pasta machine. (Never wet your pasta machine.)

Silicone-coated tongs are handy for tossing and turning the pasta; these are more gentle than metal tongs.

Specialised equipment

For someone who makes pasta often, more specialised equipment will make the process speedier.

Electric pasta machines are more expensive and much heavier than hand-cranked models, but the motor does the work, so you just have to hold and feed the dough through. They are also handy when cutting pasta — the cutting attachments are again driven by the motor.

Ravioli attachments are available for both hand-cranked and motorised machines. You put filling in the top, feed the pasta sheets through and a rotating mould shapes and seals the ravioli.

Ravioli tray moulds are specialised trays: you lay a pasta sheet in the tray, place spoonfuls of filling on top, place another pasta sheet on top then roll over the surface with a rolling pin to seal the ravioli.

Specialised electric machines are available; some motorised machines mix the eggs and flour and have various nozzles that can be attached. The machine then extrudes the dough through the nozzles to make short pasta shapes such as penne. The dough recipes with these machines are quite specific, as the dough needs to be firm.

Pasta bikes are rollers to help cut multiple strands of pasta perfectly.

Fluted pastry wheel cutters are used when cutting ravioli, to give a wavy edge.

Pasta drying racks are multiple rods that fan out around a tripod stand, so you can dry pasta in a compact way on the work surface.

Pasta forks are used to serve long pasta such as spaghetti.

Basic pasta dough

When making pasta dough, use '00' flour, a very finely ground flour with a high gluten content, which helps with the structure of the pasta. Kneading adds strength to the pasta so that it holds up well during cooking. Resting is also essential, as it reduces the chance of shrinkage as you roll and cook the pasta. This quantity is enough to serve four as a main and eight as a starter.

PREPARATION TIME 20 minutes
(+ 1 hour resting)
MAKES 600 g (1 lb 6 oz)

375 g (13 oz/2½ cups) '00' flour,
    plus extra
1 teaspoon salt
3 eggs, at room temperature
3–4 egg yolks,
    at room temperature
3 teaspoons olive oil

1   Sift the flour and salt together onto a clean work surface and make a well in the centre (*pic 1*).

2   Crack the eggs into a measuring jug. Add the yolks one at a time — you're aiming for 220 ml (7½ fl oz) of egg and egg yolk in total (you may not need all of the yolks). Measuring ensures accuracy and helps if you are using organic eggs, which are often different sizes (*pic 2*).

3   Measure the olive oil. Pour the eggs and the olive oil into the well in the flour (*pic 3*). Use the fingertips of one hand to break up the yolks, then move your fingers in a circular motion, gradually incorporating the flour. Then use both hands to bring it together into a rough dough (*pic 4*).

4   Knead for 8 minutes or until the dough is smooth and elastic (*pic 5*). Divide the dough into two equal portions (*pic 6*), shape into balls and cover with a slightly damp cloth.

Stand at room temperature for 1 hour before rolling and cutting.

VARIATIONS

Spinach pasta: Blanch 250 g (9 oz) trimmed English spinach leaves in boiling water until just wilted and bright green. Drain and refresh under cold running water. Use your hands and then a cloth to squeeze out any excess water. Then use a food processor to finely chop the spinach. Add to the flour with the eggs. As you knead the dough the spinach will be speckled throughout it. Once it has rested and you roll the dough, the rolling process will distribute the spinach evenly through the pasta. When putting the dough through the machine, after step 6 (see pages 10–11), repeat steps 5–6 to help distribute the spinach.

Herb pasta: Add 2 tablespoons freshly chopped flat-leaf (Italian) parsley to the flour with the eggs.

Tomato pasta: Add 1½ tablespoons tomato paste (concentrated purée) to the flour with the eggs; you may need to dust the pasta with flour as you knead, as it adds extra moisture, which can make the dough sticky.

Saffron pasta: Finely chop 1 teaspoon saffron threads and add to the flour with the eggs.

Chilli pasta: Add 1 teaspoon dried chilli flakes to the flour with the eggs.

Lemon and black pepper pasta: Add the finely grated zest of 2 lemons and ¼ teaspoon freshly ground black pepper (not too coarse, otherwise it will interfere with rolling) to the flour with the eggs.

Black pepper pasta: Add 1 teaspoon freshly ground black pepper (not too coarse, otherwise it will interfere with rolling) to the flour with the eggs.

TIP If you prefer, you can make pasta dough in a food processor. Place the flour and salt in the bowl of a food processor, add the egg mixture and pulse until well combined. Turn onto a lightly floured surface and knead until a smooth dough forms. Knead for a further 7 minutes or until smooth and elastic. Continue with step 4 (see left).

1 Sift the flour and salt together onto a clean work surface and make a well in the centre.

2 Measure 220 ml (7½ fl oz) whole eggs and egg yolks, adding one yolk at a time.

3 Pour the eggs and oil into the well in the flour.

4 Once all the liquid has been incorporated, a rough dough should form.

5 Continue kneading until the dough is smooth and elastic.

6 Cut the dough into two equal portions, cover with a slightly damp cloth and rest at room temperature for 1 hour.

Rolling fresh pasta dough

Rolling out your own pasta might seem like a challenge if you've never done it before, but give it a try — you could get the kids involved as well. It's fun, and the reward of eating your own fresh pasta is the motivation! Find a recipe using fresh pasta in the next chapter then decide if you want to flavour the dough (see page 8) and what shape you are going to cut it, so you are all organised. Ensure that you have a large enough work surface for the sheets. Follow these steps to help you get the feel for the process.

1 Set a pasta machine on the thickest setting. (Note: it is a good idea to attach the cutter attachment to the pasta machine even when just rolling sheets of pasta — it helps to support the pasta.) Dust one portion of the dough very lightly with flour, then use a rolling pin to roll out to the thickness of the widest setting of your pasta machine (*pic 1*). Keep the other ball of dough covered with a slightly damp cloth until needed.

2 Feed the dough into the rollers. Use one hand to turn the handle and the other hand to support the dough as it comes through the roller (*pic 2*). If the pasta doesn't come through cleanly and evenly, fold it into thirds, turn it 90 degrees and pass it through again.

3 Pass the dough through the machine one or two more times until about 70 cm (28 inches) long (*pic 3*), lightly dusting with flour if necessary and reducing the roller setting by one notch after each rolling. This process both rolls the pasta into sheets and works the gluten in the wheat to give the pasta a firm, strong texture.

4 Return the machine to the thickest setting. Fold the dough back on itself in half (*pic 4*) and pass it, open end first, through the machine. Then pass the dough through one or two more times, reducing the roller setting by one notch each time. When the pasta is about 80 cm (32 inches) long, cut it in half widthways. Lay one portion of dough flat on the work surface and cover with a slightly damp cloth while you continue working with the other half.

5 Return the machine to the thickest setting. Fold one half of the pasta into thirds and use a rolling pin to roll it out to the thickness of the widest setting of your pasta machine (*pic 5*). Keep in mind not to roll the piece too wide — it should be about 1 cm (½ inch) less than the width of your rollers as you want the finished sheet to gradually get wider as you roll. This is important for making ravioli and other filled pastas.

6 Pass the dough, open end first, through the rollers (*pic 6*). (Turning the dough and passing it through the rollers at a different angle gives strength and elasticity to the pasta.)

7 Continue to pass the dough through the pasta machine, dusting lightly with flour as necessary and reducing the roller setting by one notch after each rolling (*pic 7*), until less than 1 mm (½₂ inch) thick (*pic 8*), (or to the thickness required in the particular recipe). You may need to cut the pasta in half at some point, depending on how much bench space you have and how easy you find the pasta to handle.

8 When the rolling is completed, the pasta should be so thin that you can see the shadow of an open-fingered hand underneath.

9 Once you have completed the rolling process, the pasta is ready for cutting or filling (*pic 9*). (If you're going to use the sheets for filled pasta, don't dust them with any more flour at this stage, as that will prevent the sheets from sticking together once filled; see page 14.)

10 Repeat the rolling and cutting or filling with the other half of the dough.

1 Roll one portion of dough to the thickness of the widest setting of the pasta machine.

2 Begin feeding the dough through the rollers, using one hand to support it.

3 Pass the dough through the rollers once or twice more.

4 Fold the dough back on itself and pass it through the machine on the widest setting.

5 Fold into thirds and roll to the thickness of the widest setting on the machine.

6 Pass the dough, open end first, through the rollers.

7 Continue to roll, reducing the roller setting by one notch after each rolling.

8 The finished dough should be thin enough to be transparent.

9 The dough is now ready to be cut and dried, or filled.

Cutting fresh pasta dough

Cutting by machine

Most pasta machines come with an attachment that cuts ribbon pastas. Generally you would have attached this already when rolling the pasta as it helps to support the pasta as you feed it through.

1 Dust the rolled-out pasta sheets quite generously with flour on both sides, and begin to feed them through the machine.

2 As the strands emerge, catch them on your hand to gently support them.

3 Discard the outer strands from cutting, as they are often uneven.

Cutting by hand

Only ribbon pastas can be cut by hand — some shapes, such as spaghetti, need to be done by machine. Don't get too carried away with neatness; a rustic look is appropriate for handcut pasta.

1 Dust a pasta sheet quite generously with flour on both sides, then cut into desired lengths. Fold several times to form a loose roll (or roll around a rolling pin), keeping the sides straight as you fold.

2 Use a large sharp knife to cut as desired: 8 mm (3/8 inch) thick for fettuccine or 2 cm (3/4 inch) thick for pappardelle.

3 Carefully unravel the pasta and dry as instructed on the following page.

Drying fresh pasta dough

You can buy pasta drying racks, but it's easy enough to improvise your own, for example by hanging ribbons of cut pasta over a clean broom handle (or length of thickish dowel) suspended between two chairs. A clothes-drying rack can also work well.

1   Rig up your pasta drying rack (see above), then hang the cut pasta over it.

2   Some pastas, such as fettuccine, can be hung to dry for an hour or so, then rolled into small nests while still pliable. This makes the pasta less likely to break during storage.

3   Place the nests on the base of a large, lightly floured airtight container and leave for 24 hours (with the lid off) to dry completely.

> **TIP** If you are making pasta to cook immediately, you can roll it out, hang it to partially dry, prepare your sauce and then cook the pasta just before you're ready to serve. Any leftover pasta should be dried completely and stored as described above.

4   Seal the container and store in a cool place for up to 1 week. You could also use a large, deep-sided tray and wrap it well in plastic wrap so it is airtight.

Shaping filled pasta

If making filled pasta, after the final roll through the machine don't sprinkle it with flour as you will need the sheets to stick together. Also be sure to press any excess air out of the pasta shape as you seal it.

Ravioli

1 Place one rolled pasta sheet on a very lightly floured surface. Keep other sheets covered. Place 1 teaspoon of filling on the pasta sheet, leaving 4 cm (1½ inches) between the mounds.

2 Brush around the filling lightly with some beaten egg. Place another pasta sheet on top, then press around the edge of the filling to enclose it, taking care to expel any air.

3 Cut into 6.5 cm (2½ inch) square ravioli using a fluted pastry wheel. Place, so they are not touching, in a single layer on a tray lined with lightly floured baking paper. Repeat with remaining dough and filling.

Agnolotti

1 Place a pasta sheet on a lightly floured surface. Cut out 6.5 cm (2½ inch) rounds. Cover the cut rounds with a clean cloth so they don't dry out.

2 Place 1 teaspoon of filling in the centre of each round and brush the edges lightly with some beaten egg.

3 Fold into a half moon, pressing the edges to seal and taking care to expel any air. Place in a single layer on a tray lined with lightly floured baking paper, ensuring the pasta edges aren't touching. Repeat with remaining dough and filling.

Tortellini

1 Place a pasta sheet on a lightly floured surface. Cut 6.5 cm (2½ inch) rounds from the pasta sheets. Cover with a clean cloth. Place ¼ teaspoon of filling in the centre of each round. Brush the edges with some beaten egg.

2 Fold into a half moon, pressing the edges to seal and expel any air. Wrap the folded side around your fingertip, brushing one edge lightly with beaten egg, and pinch to seal.

3 Place, so they are not touching, in a single layer on a tray lined with lightly floured baking paper.

TIP Make two or more batches of filled pasta so you can freeze what you don't cook. To prevent the filled pasta sticking together when frozen, place them, so they don't touch each other, on a large tray lined with baking paper that will fit inside your freezer, and freeze. When they are nearly frozen, pack them into an airtight container or a ziplock bag and return to the freezer. It's a good idea to use the frozen filled pasta within 1 month. There's no need to thaw the frozen filled pasta, simply cook in boiling salted water for a few minutes more than specified in the recipe, until the filling is cooked, the pasta al dente and the pasta floats to the top.

How much to serve?

It's easy to cook more or less pasta than you need if you don't measure it. Kitchen scales are readily available and take the guesswork out of cooking. The quantities below are general guidelines for how much pasta to serve.

Dried pasta per person
60 g (2¼ oz) as a starter
100–125 g (3½–4½ oz) as a main

Fresh pasta per person
70 g (2½ oz) as a starter
150 g (5½ oz) as a main

Fresh filled pasta per person
100 g (3½ oz) as a starter
200 g (7 oz) as a main

Cooking pasta

Use a large saucepan or stockpot filled with plenty of water so that the pasta has space to move about. There's no need to add oil to the water, or to rinse pasta before serving (see below). Reserve some of the cooking water to add to your sauce if it needs thinning.

Fresh pasta

For each 600 g (1 lb 5 oz) fresh pasta or 800 g (1 lb 12 oz) filled pasta, use 6 litres (210 fl oz/24 cups) water and 1 tablespoon salt. Unfilled fresh pasta cooks very quickly. Refer to specific recipes for filled pasta, which will generally need to cook for longer (it is very important that meat fillings are cooked completely).

1 Bring the water to the boil in a large deep saucepan over high heat, add the salt and return the water to the boil.

2 Add the pasta to the water, stir gently and cook until al dente (see below). Unfilled fresh pasta is generally cooked by the time the water returns to the boil, so keep an eye on it.

3 Drain in a small-holed colander, with a large bowl beneath it to capture the cooking water. Remove the colander from the bowl and drain. Reserve some of the cooking water.

Pasta perfection

Al dente ('to the bite') is how Italians describe the texture of well-cooked pasta. Test pasta towards the end of cooking; it should feel slightly elastic and you should feel a little resistance as you bite the pasta (or break it using your thumb); however, it should not be at all chalky in the centre.

Timing is the difference between a good pasta meal and a great one. Read the recipe through first and coordinate your cooking times. Have the table set, parmesan cheese (if using) grated and the serving bowls warmed. Aim to have the sauce ready to dress the pasta as soon as it is cooked, especially for fresh pasta, which will continue to cook slightly even once drained.

Draining It is important to add the pasta to the sauce after draining. Don't overdrain the pasta or shake it too vigorously in the colander — it needs to be slippery for the sauce to coat it well. Never leave cooked pasta sitting in the colander for long — fresh pasta, especially, can become a sticky mass.

Rinsing The only times you might rinse pasta is if you are going to serve it cold, or when blanching fresh sheets for lasagne. Rinse it under cold water or place in a bowl of iced water to arrest the cooking, then drain and toss it in a little oil to prevent it from sticking together. Cover and refrigerate if not using immediately.

Dried pasta

For four people, you will need 500 g (1 lb 2 oz) dried pasta as a main. For this quantity of dried pasta, you will need 5 litres (175 fl oz/20 cups) water and 1 tablespoon salt. Most commercial dried pastas cook in about 11 minutes, but always check the directions on the packet and begin testing a minute or two before the end of the recommended cooking time.

1 Bring the water to the boil in a large deep saucepan over high heat, add the salt and return the water to the boil.

2 Add the pasta, stirring to avoid it sticking together. Gently bend long pasta (such as spaghetti or fettuccine) as you add it and stir as it softens so it is covered by the water. Cover with a lid briefly until it returns to the boil (don't let it boil over).

3 Cook until al dente. The pasta should be al dente (firm to the bite but have no chalkiness in the centre). Once cooked, drain as described in step 3 (opposite), reserving some of the cooking water.

Classics

Italian meatballs with spaghetti

The addition of milk-soaked bread helps to keep the meatballs moist. To get the most flavour in your meatballs, don't roll the balls too tightly. This allows the sauce to soak into the meatballs during cooking. Spaghetti is traditional, but other long pastas will work well too.

SERVES 4   **PREPARATION TIME** 30 minutes   **COOKING TIME** 1 hour 15 minutes

80 g (2¾ oz) day-old white
   bread, finely chopped
   (about 3 slices)
125 ml (4 fl oz/½ cup) milk
60 ml (2 fl oz/¼ cup) olive oil
1 brown onion, finely chopped
100 g (3½ oz) pancetta, finely
   chopped
2 garlic cloves, crushed
125 ml (4 fl oz/½ cup) red wine
500 g (1 lb 2 oz) minced (ground)
   beef
300 g (10½ oz) mixed minced
   (ground) pork and veal
50 g (1¾ oz/½ cup) finely grated
   pecorino cheese
700 g (1 lb 9 oz) tomato passata
   (puréed tomatoes)
250 ml (9 fl oz/1 cup) chicken stock
400 g (14 oz) dried spaghetti or
   600 g (1 lb 5 oz) fresh spaghetti
   (see pages 8–13)
grated parmesan cheese, to serve

1   Preheat the oven to 180°C (350°F/ Gas 4). Combine the bread and milk in a small bowl and stand for 10 minutes or until softened (*pic 1*).

2   Meanwhile, heat 1 tablespoon of the oil in a frying pan over medium heat. Add the onion, pancetta and garlic and cook, stirring, for 5–10 minutes or until softened. Add the wine and bring to the boil. Reduce the heat to low and simmer for 3 minutes or until almost completely evaporated. Transfer to a bowl and allow to cool to room temperature.

3   Combine the bread mixture, onion mixture, meats and cheese in a large bowl. Season with salt and freshly ground black pepper, then mix well.

4   Use wet hands to roll heaped tablespoons of the meat mixture into 25 balls (*pic 2*). Place in a large baking dish (the meatballs need to fit fairly snugly in the dish).

5   Heat the remaining oil in a large frying pan over medium heat. Add the tomato passata and stock. Bring to the boil. Reduce the heat to low and simmer, uncovered, for 20 minutes or until reduced slightly.

6   Pour the tomato sauce mixture over the meatballs (*pic 3*). Cover the dish with foil and bake for 45 minutes.

7   Cook the pasta in a large saucepan of boiling salted water, following the packet instructions, until al dente. Drain and return to the pan. Add some of the sauce and toss to combine. Serve the spaghetti topped with the meatballs, sauce and parmesan cheese.

1

2

3

Macaroni cheese

This comforting family standby never falls out of favour. Keep it plain for the kids if that's how they like it, or glam it up a bit for the adults by replacing some of the tasty cheese with blue cheese or another strong-flavoured variety, or even a combination of types.

SERVES 6 **PREPARATION TIME** 15 minutes **COOKING TIME** 50 minutes

300 g (10½ oz) dried macaroni
2 slices country or sourdough bread,
    crusts trimmed
50 g (1¾ oz) butter
35 g (1¼ oz/¼ cup) plain
    (all-purpose) flour
875 ml (30 fl oz/3½ cups) milk
1 tablespoon dijon mustard
1 egg yolk
125 g (4½ oz/1¼ cups) grated
    tasty cheese
2 tablespoons chopped flat-leaf
    (Italian) parsley
1½ tablespoons olive oil, to drizzle
green salad, to serve

1   Preheat the oven to 180°C (350°F/ Gas 4).

2   Cook the pasta in a large saucepan of boiling salted water, following the packet instructions, until al dente. Drain well. Process the bread into coarse crumbs by pulsing it in a food processor (*pic 1*).

3   Meanwhile, melt the butter in a saucepan over medium–high heat. When the butter starts to sizzle, stir in the flour and cook, stirring, for 1 minute or until pale and bubbly. Remove from the heat and slowly stir in the milk until smooth (*pic 2*). Return to the heat and cook, stirring, until the mixture starts to boil and thicken. Remove from the heat and whisk in the mustard and egg yolk. Stand for 5 minutes to cool slightly, then stir in

the cheese until smooth. Stir in the pasta and season well with salt and freshly ground black pepper (*pic 3*).

4   Spoon the pasta mixture into six 375 ml (13 fl oz/1½ cup) ovenproof ramekins. Put the breadcrumbs and parsley in a bowl, drizzle with the oil and toss to combine. Sprinkle evenly over the pasta mixture (depending on the width of the ramekins, you may need less breadcrumbs). Bake for 35 minutes or until golden. Serve with a green salad.

VARIATIONS

Basil and pine nut: Omit the mustard. Replace the tasty cheese with a shredded four-cheese blend (usually a blend of cheddar, parmesan and two types of mozzarella, available from supermarkets). Stir in ½ cup roughly chopped fresh basil and 60 ml (2 fl oz/ ¼ cup) freshly squeezed lemon juice along with the pasta. Sprinkle over 40 g (1½ oz/¼ cup) pine nuts along with the breadcrumbs.

Chargrilled capsicum and olive: Omit the mustard. Replace the tasty cheese with a shredded four-cheese blend (usually a blend of cheddar, parmesan and two types of mozzarella, available from supermarkets). Stir in 250 g (9 oz) roughly chopped chargrilled capsicum (pepper) and 30 g (1 oz/½ cup) small pitted black olives, quartered, along with the pasta.

TIP You can also bake this dish in a greased 2.25 litre (80 fl oz) ovenproof dish, measuring about 18 x 30 x 6 cm (7 x 12 x 2½ inches).

Minestrone

Begin this recipe a day ahead, as the beans need soaking overnight. Or, for a quicker version, use two tins of beans — borlotti or cannellini are suitable. Rinse them well before use and add them in step 4, with the carrot, swede and potato.

SERVES 6–8 **PREPARATION TIME** 15 minutes (+ overnight soaking) **COOKING TIME** 3 hours

200 g (7 oz/1 cup) dried
   borlotti beans
2 tablespoons olive oil
2 brown onions, chopped
2 garlic cloves, crushed
3 bacon rashers, chopped
4 roma (plum) tomatoes,
   peeled and chopped
¼ cup chopped flat-leaf
   (Italian) parsley
2.25 litres (80 fl oz) beef
   or vegetable stock
60 ml (2 fl oz/¼ cup) red wine
1 carrot, chopped
1 swede, diced
2 potatoes, diced
3 tablespoons tomato paste
   (concentrated purée)
50 g (1¾ oz/⅓ cup) fresh
   or frozen peas
2 zucchini (courgettes), halved
   and sliced
80 g (2¾ oz/½ cup) dried small
   macaroni
pesto (see page 33) and grated
   parmesan cheese, to serve
   (optional)

1 Soak the beans in water overnight (*pic 1*).

2 Drain and rinse the beans and place in a large saucepan. Cover with cold water. Bring to the boil, stir, then lower the heat and simmer for 15 minutes. Drain.

3 Heat the oil in a large saucepan over medium heat and cook the onion, garlic and bacon, stirring, until the onion is soft and the bacon is lightly browned (*pic 2*).

4 Add the beans, tomato, parsley, stock and wine. Cover and simmer over low heat for 2 hours. Add the carrot, swede, potato and tomato paste and simmer, covered, for 20 minutes. Add the peas, zucchini and pasta (*pic 3*). Cover and simmer for 10–15 minutes or until the vegetables and pasta are tender. Season with salt and freshly ground black pepper, and serve topped with a little pesto and grated parmesan cheese, if desired.

1

2

3

> **TIP** If using frozen peas, there's no need to thaw them before adding them to the soup.

Amatriciana pasta

This spicy bacon and tomato sauce is believed to have originated in the town of Amatrice, where bacon is a prized local product. Traditionally, bucatini is used with this sauce, but you can use any pasta you prefer — we've used strozzapreti or you could use casarecce or fusilli.

SERVES 4 **PREPARATION TIME** 45 minutes **COOKING TIME** 20 minutes

6 thin pancetta slices or
  3 bacon rashers
1 kg (2 lb 4 oz) very ripe tomatoes
500 g (1 lb 2 oz) dried strozzapreti
  or fusilli pasta
1 tablespoon olive oil
1 small onion, very finely chopped
2 teaspoons very finely chopped
  small red chilli
shaved parmesan cheese, to serve
  (optional)

1 Finely chop the pancetta or bacon. Score a cross in the base of each tomato. Soak the tomatoes in boiling water for 1–2 minutes, drain and plunge into cold water briefly. Peel back the skin from the cross. Halve, remove the seeds and chop the flesh.

2 Cook the pasta in a large saucepan of boiling salted water, following the packet instructions, until al dente. Drain and return to the pan.

3 About 5 minutes before the pasta is cooked, heat the oil in a heavy-based frying pan over medium heat. Add the pancetta or bacon, onion and chilli and stir for 3 minutes. Add the tomato and season with salt and freshly ground black pepper. Reduce the heat and simmer for 3 minutes. Add the sauce to the pasta and toss until well combined. Garnish with the cheese, if desired, and pepper.

> **TIP** For a change from regular tomatoes, you can try roma (plum) tomatoes. They are firm-fleshed, with few seeds and have a rich flavour when cooked.

Pasta marinara

The key to making marinara sauce is to keep a close eye on the cooking of the seafood. You want it to be just cooked through, so once it's done remove the pan from the heat and serve immediately.

SERVES 4 **PREPARATION TIME** 20 minutes **COOKING TIME** 40 minutes

50 ml (1¾ fl oz) extra virgin olive oil
1 large brown onion, finely chopped
4 garlic cloves, crushed
2½ tablespoons tomato paste (concentrated purée)
375 ml (13 fl oz/1½ cups) white wine
700 ml (24 fl oz) tomato passata (puréed tomatoes)
4 sprigs oregano, plus leaves, to garnish
large pinch white sugar
16 black mussels, scrubbed and beards removed
400 g (14 oz) dried spaghetti or 600 g (1 lb 5 oz) fresh spaghetti (see pages 8–13)
300 g (10½ oz) firm white skinless fish fillets, cut into 2.5 cm (1 inch) pieces
200 g (7 oz) raw prawns (shrimp), peeled and deveined, leaving the tails intact
200 g (7 oz) scallop meat

1   Heat the oil in a large saucepan over medium–low heat. Add the onion and garlic and cook, stirring, for 8 minutes or until softened. Add the tomato paste and cook, stirring, for 2 minutes, then add the wine. Bring to the boil and cook for about 5 minutes or until the liquid has reduced slightly. Add the tomato passata, oregano sprigs and sugar. Bring the mixture to a simmer then reduce the heat to low and cook for 20 minutes or until reduced and slightly thickened. Discard the oregano (*pic 1*).

2   Meanwhile, bring 125 ml (4 fl oz/ ½ cup) water to the boil in a medium saucepan, add the mussels and cook over medium–high heat, shaking the pan occasionally, for 4–5 minutes or until the mussels have opened (*pic 2*). Remove the mussels from the pan, discarding any that have not opened. Add 2–3 tablespoons of the mussel cooking liquid to the tomato sauce to thin it slightly.

3   Cook the pasta in a large saucepan of boiling salted water, following the packet instructions, until al dente. Drain well.

4   Meanwhile, add the fish, prawns and scallops to the hot sauce (*pic 3*), cover the pan and cook over medium heat for 5 minutes or until just cooked through. Add the mussels and heat through. Divide the pasta among warmed bowls, then spoon over the sauce and scatter with the oregano leaves to serve.

1

2

3

TIP You can vary the seafood according to your preference or what is in season – use clams, pipis, thin slices of calamari or scampi (or chunks of lobster or other crayfish for a touch of luxury).

Lasagne

There are several versions of a traditional Italian meat sauce for lasagne and they vary depending on the region of origin. Here, as is the custom in the north, full-cream milk is added to the sauce for richness. Simmering the sauce over low heat for a long time adds extra intensity to the flavour.

SERVES 8   **PREPARATION TIME** 20 minutes (+ 10 minutes standing)   **COOKING TIME** 2 hours 45 minutes

60 ml (2 fl oz/¼ cup) olive oil
1 brown onion, chopped
1 celery stalk, finely chopped
1 carrot, finely chopped
600 g (1 lb 5 oz) mixed minced (ground) pork and veal
2 teaspoons mixed dried Italian herbs
4 garlic cloves, chopped
250 ml (9 fl oz/1 cup) milk
375 ml (13 fl oz/1½ cups) red wine
400 g (14 oz) tin chopped tomatoes
2 tablespoons tomato paste (concentrated purée)
250 ml (9 fl oz/1 cup) good-quality chicken stock
50 g (1¾ oz) butter, chopped
300 g (10½ oz) fresh lasagne sheets (see pages 8–10)
125 g (4½ oz) finely grated parmesan cheese
¼ cup basil leaves, to serve

BÉCHAMEL SAUCE
125 g (4½ oz) butter, chopped
125 g (4½ oz) plain (all-purpose) flour
1 litre (35 fl oz/4 cups) warm milk
1 bay leaf

1   Heat the oil in a large saucepan over low heat and cook the onion, celery and carrot for 5 minutes or until soft (*pic 1*).

2   Add the meat to pan and stir over medium heat for 5 minutes. Stir in the herbs and garlic.

3   Add the milk (*pic 2*), stir and cook over low heat for 10 minutes, stirring occasionally or until the milk is absorbed.

4   Stir in the wine, tomatoes, tomato paste and stock and simmer over low heat for 1½ hours or until thick (add a little hot water if the mixture is sticking). Season with salt and pepper.

5   Meanwhile, make the béchamel sauce. Melt the butter in a saucepan over low heat. Add the flour and whisk until the mixture is dry and grainy. Gradually whisk in the warm milk and bring to a simmer. Add the bay leaf and cook for 5 minutes, whisking occasionally, until thick. Season, cover with plastic wrap and cool slightly. Remove bay leaf.

6   Preheat the oven to 180°C (350°F/ Gas 4).

7   Rub half the butter over the base of a 3 litre (105 fl oz) casserole dish, measuring about 19 x 35 x 7.5 cm (7½ x 14 x 3 inches) and line the base with pasta. Top with one-third of the meat sauce and one-third of the béchamel sauce. Top with another layer of pasta (*pic 3*). Continue layering (you will have three layers of pasta), finishing with a layer of béchamel sauce. Sprinkle with the cheese and dot with remaining butter.

8   Bake for 45 minutes or until browned and bubbling. Remove from the oven and stand for 10 minutes; scatter with the basil to serve.

1

2

3

Top 10 simple pasta dishes

All of these sauces are for 500 g (1 lb 2 oz) dried pasta, 600 g (1 lb 5 oz) fresh pasta or 800 g (1 lb 12 oz) filled pasta.

Pomodoro/Napolitana pasta

SERVES 4
PREPARATION TIME 10 minutes
COOKING TIME 30 minutes

2 tablespoons olive oil
1 brown onion, finely chopped
2 garlic cloves, finely chopped
2 tablespoons finely chopped flat-leaf (Italian) parsley
2 x 400 g (14 oz) tins chopped tomatoes, or 1 kg (2 lb 4 oz) fresh tomatoes, peeled and chopped
1 tablespoon tomato paste (concentrated purée)
1 teaspoon white sugar
500 g (1 lb 2 oz) dried pasta or 600 g (1 lb 5 oz) fresh pasta (such as bucatini) (see pages 8–13)
¼ cup shredded basil
grated parmesan cheese, to serve

1 Heat the oil in a large frying pan over low heat. Add the onion, garlic and parsley and cook for 3 minutes or until the onion is soft.

2 Add the tomatoes, tomato paste and sugar. Partially cover and simmer for 30 minutes or until the sauce thickens. Season with salt and freshly ground black pepper.

3 Cook the pasta in a large saucepan of boiling salted water, following the packet instructions, until al dente. Drain, toss with the sauce, garnish with the basil and serve with the cheese.

Alfredo pasta

SERVES 4
PREPARATION TIME 5 minutes
COOKING TIME 10 minutes

50 g (1¾ oz) butter
300 ml (10½ fl oz) thin (pouring) cream
500 g (1 lb 2 oz) dried pasta or 600 g (1 lb 5 oz) fresh pasta (such as fettuccine) (see pages 8–13)
85 g (3 oz) finely grated parmesan cheese
pinch freshly grated nutmeg
2 tablespoons finely chopped flat-leaf (Italian) parsley

1 Heat the butter and 200 ml (7 fl oz) of the cream in a large frying pan over low heat. Simmer for 6 minutes.

2 Meanwhile, cook the pasta in a large saucepan of boiling salted water, following the packet instructions, until al dente. Drain and return to the pan.

3 Add the warmed cream to the pasta and toss well to coat. Add the remaining cream, the cheese, nutmeg and parsley and season with salt and pepper. Toss again, then serve.

Carrettierra pasta

SERVES 4
PREPARATION TIME 5 minutes
COOKING TIME 10 minutes

60 g (2¼ oz/1 cup lightly packed) day-old Italian breadcrumbs
125 ml (4 fl oz/½ cup) olive oil
1 large brown onion, finely chopped
2–3 garlic cloves, finely chopped
½ teaspoon dried oregano
500 g (1 lb 2 oz) dried pasta or 600 g (1 lb 5 oz) fresh pasta (such as spaghetti) (see pages 8–13)
⅓ cup finely chopped flat-leaf (Italian) parsley

1 Spread the breadcrumbs on a baking tray and grill (broil) for 2 minutes or until lightly toasted. Heat the oil in a large frying pan over medium heat. Cook the onion, garlic and oregano for 5 minutes or until soft.

2 Cook the pasta in a large saucepan of boiling salted water, following the packet instructions, until al dente. Drain. Stir the breadcrumbs and parsley through the onion mixture and season with salt and pepper. Toss through the pasta.

Four-cheese pasta

SERVES 4
PREPARATION TIME 10 minutes
COOKING TIME 10 minutes

300 ml (10½ fl oz) thin
    (pouring) cream
85 g (3 oz) finely grated
    parmesan cheese
500 g (1 lb 2 oz) dried pasta
    or 600 g (1 lb 5 oz) fresh pasta
    (see pages 8–13)
50 g (1¾ oz) butter, diced
60 g (2¼ oz/½ cup) coarsely
    grated fontina cheese
45 g (1½ oz/⅓ cup) crumbled
    gorgonzola cheese
60 g (2¼ oz/½ cup) coarsely grated
    provolone cheese

1 Heat the cream and half of the
parmesan in a small saucepan over
low heat. Stir just to combine and
keep warm while you cook the pasta.

2 Cook the pasta in a large saucepan
of boiling salted water, following the
packet instructions, until al dente.
Drain and return to the pan.

3 Add the butter, the remaining
parmesan, the fontina, gorgonzola
and provolone to the pasta, then stir
to combine. Add the cream sauce and
toss well so the pasta is evenly coated.
Season with salt and freshly ground
black pepper, then serve.

Pesto pasta

SERVES 4
PREPARATION TIME 15 minutes
COOKING TIME 10 minutes

500 g (1 lb 2 oz) dried pasta
    or 600 g (1 lb 5 oz) fresh pasta
    (such as linguine)
    (see pages 8–13)

PESTO
100 g (3½ oz/2 cups, firmly packed)
    basil leaves, chopped
2 garlic cloves
40 g (1½ oz/¼ cup) pine nuts
70 g (2½ oz/½ cup) finely grated
    parmesan cheese, plus extra,
    to serve
185 ml (6 fl oz/¾ cup) olive oil

1 To make the pesto, combine
the basil, garlic and pine nuts in a
food processor. Add the cheese and
combine briefly. With the motor
running, add the oil in a steady
stream until mixed to a smooth paste.
Season with salt and freshly ground
black pepper. Makes 1¼ cups.

2 Cook the pasta in a large saucepan
of boiling salted water, following the
packet instructions, until al dente.
Drain and return to the pan. Toss
with the pesto, sprinkle with the extra
cheese and serve.

> **TIP** When a pesto (including the
> cheese) is stored for any length
> of time, the composition of the
> ingredients alters. The cheese
> component reacts with other
> ingredients, in particular the basil,
> and starts to turn rancid. It will
> keep, at best, for 5–7 seven days,
> if refrigerated in an airtight jar with
> a layer of olive oil or plastic wrap
> covering the exposed surface.
>
> A more successful option when
> making pesto to store is to leave
> out the cheese and stir it through
> when the sauce is ready to be
> used. In this way, your pesto will
> keep for 2–3 months refrigerated,
> or 5–6 months frozen.

Puttanesca pasta

SERVES 4
PREPARATION TIME 15 minutes
COOKING TIME 25 minutes

2 tablespoons olive oil
2–3 garlic cloves, finely chopped
1 small red chilli, finely chopped
2 x 400 g (14 oz) tins chopped
    tomatoes
1 tablespoon tomato paste
    (concentrated purée)
500 g (1 lb 2 oz) dried pasta
    or 600 g (1 lb 5 oz) fresh pasta
    (such as spaghetti, bucatini or
    linguine) (see pages 8–13)
3–4 anchovies, drained and finely
    chopped
2 tablespoons capers, rinsed,
    drained and chopped
10 kalamata olives, pitted and sliced
¼ cup chopped flat-leaf (Italian)
    parsley

1   Heat the oil in a large frying pan
over low heat, add the garlic and
chilli and cook for 2 minutes. Add
the tomatoes and tomato paste. Cook,
stirring occasionally, for 20 minutes
or until the sauce thickens.

2   Cook the pasta in a large saucepan
of boiling salted water, following the
packet instructions, until al dente.
Drain and return to the pan.

3   Meanwhile, add the anchovies,
capers and olives to the sauce, stir,
then simmer for 5 minutes.

4   Stir through the parsley and
season with freshly ground black
pepper. Toss with the pasta and serve
immediately.

Walnut and garlic pasta

SERVES 4
PREPARATION TIME 10 minutes
COOKING TIME 10 minutes

500 g (1 lb 2 oz) dried pasta
    or 600 g (1 lb 5 oz) fresh pasta
    (such as fettuccine)
    (see pages 8–13)
125 ml (4 fl oz/½ cup) extra virgin
    olive oil
150 g (5½ oz/1¼ cups) walnuts,
    roughly chopped
2–3 garlic cloves, finely chopped
60 g (2¼ oz/1 cup lightly packed)
    day-old white breadcrumbs
¼ cup finely chopped flat-leaf
    (Italian) parsley
grated parmesan cheese, to serve

1   Cook the pasta in a large saucepan
of boiling salted water, following the
packet instructions, until al dente.
Drain and return to the pan.

2   Heat the oil in a large frying
pan over medium heat and add the
walnuts, garlic and breadcrumbs.

3   Reduce the heat and cook for
2 minutes or until the walnuts and
breadcrumbs are lightly golden —
take care not to brown them too much
or the walnuts will be bitter. Sprinkle
with the parsley and season with salt
and freshly ground black pepper. Toss
the walnut mixture through the pasta.
Sprinkle with the cheese to serve.

Carbonara pasta

SERVES 4
PREPARATION TIME 10 minutes
COOKING TIME 10 minutes

3 eggs, lightly beaten
125 ml (4 fl oz/½ cup) thin
    (pouring) cream
100 g (3½ oz/¾ cup) grated
    parmesan cheese
500 g (1 lb 2 oz) dried pasta
    or 600 g (1 lb 5 oz) fresh pasta
    (such as linguine, tagliatelle or
    fettuccine) (see pages 8–13)
2 tablespoons olive oil
2 garlic cloves, finely chopped
6 bacon rashers, chopped

1   Combine the egg, cream and
cheese in a bowl and set aside.

2   Cook the pasta in a large saucepan
of boiling salted water, following the
packet instructions, until al dente.
Drain well.

3   Heat the oil in a large, deep frying
pan over medium heat. Add the garlic
and bacon and cook for 3–4 minutes
or until the bacon is just crisp (take
care not to burn it).

4   Add the pasta to the frying pan
and toss well. Remove from the heat
and stir through the egg mixture.
Season with freshly ground black
pepper and serve immediately.

> **TIP** The heat of the pasta will cook
> the egg. Don't be tempted to leave
> the pan on the heat or the egg will
> scramble.

Garlic and chilli pasta

SERVES 4
PREPARATION TIME 10 minutes
COOKING TIME 10 minutes

500 g (1 lb 2 oz) dried pasta
or 600 g (1 lb 5 oz) fresh pasta
(such as spaghettini or linguine)
(see pages 8–13)
125 ml (4 fl oz/½ cup) extra virgin
olive oil
2–3 garlic cloves, finely chopped
1–2 small red chillies, seeded and
finely chopped
¼ cup finely chopped flat-leaf
(Italian) parsley

1   Cook the pasta in a large saucepan
of boiling salted water, following the
packet instructions, until al dente.
Drain and return to the pan.

2   Meanwhile, heat the oil in a frying
pan over low heat. Add the garlic and
chilli and cook for 2–3 minutes or
until the garlic is golden. Take care not
to burn the garlic or chilli, or the sauce
will have a bitter taste.

3   Toss the parsley and oil mixture
through the pasta and season with salt
and freshly ground black pepper.

Butter and sage pasta

SERVES 4
PREPARATION TIME 5 minutes
COOKING TIME 10 minutes

500 g (1 lb 2 oz) dried pasta,
or 600 g (1 lb 5 oz) fresh
pasta   (such as spaghetti or
linguine) (see pages 8–13), or
800 g (1 lb 12 oz) ravioli filled
with spinach and ricotta or
pumpkin (see pages 8–14)
100 g (3½ oz) butter, chopped
⅔ cup sage leaves
shaved parmesan cheese, to serve

1   Cook the pasta in a large saucepan
of boiling salted water, following the
packet instructions, until al dente.
Drain and return to the pan.

2   Meanwhile, heat a small saucepan
over medium–high heat. Add the
butter and cook for 4–6 minutes until
it is foamy and nut brown.

3   Remove the butter from the heat,
add the sage leaves, stir to combine,
then toss with the pasta and serve,
sprinkled with the cheese.

Matching sauces to pasta shapes

There are good reasons for
matching a certain pasta shape
with a particular sauce. Apart from
the traditional regional preference
for a particular shape, its ability
to hold and support sauce is all
important. Tubular shapes such as
penne capture thick sauces, while
flat or long pastas are traditionally
served with thin, smooth sauce.
Imagine the texture and flavour of
the sauce – light sauces go with
delicate pasta shapes and robust
sauces with sturdy shapes. But
there are no hard and fast rules
and with many shapes and flavours
available it is fun to experiment.

Creamy boscaiola

There's a good reason why this delicious sauce is a classic. The combination of smoky bacon with rich cream is irresistible. Boscaiola means woodcutter in Italian – collecting mushrooms is part of the heritage of the woodcutters.

SERVES 4   **PREPARATION TIME** 15 minutes   **COOKING TIME** 25 minutes

500 g (1 lb 2 oz) dried long pasta or
   600 g (1 lb 5 oz) fresh long pasta
   (see pages 8–13)
1 tablespoon olive oil
6 bacon rashers, roughly chopped
200 g (7 oz) button mushrooms,
   sliced
625 ml (21½ fl oz/2½ cups)
   thin (pouring) cream
2 spring onions (scallions), sliced
1 tablespoon chopped flat-leaf
   (Italian) parsley

1   Cook the pasta in a large saucepan of boiling salted water, following the packet instructions, until al dente. Drain, return to the pan and keep warm.

2   Meanwhile, heat the oil in a large frying pan, add the bacon and mushroom and cook, stirring, for 5 minutes or until golden brown.

3   Stir in a little of the cream (*pic 1*) and scrape the wooden spoon on the bottom of the pan to dislodge any bacon that has stuck.

4   Add the remaining cream, bring to the boil and cook over high heat for 15 minutes or until the sauce is thick enough to coat the back of the spoon (*pic 2*). Stir the spring onion through the mixture. Pour the sauce over the pasta and toss to combine. Serve sprinkled with the parsley.

1

2

TIP This sauce is normally served with spaghetti, but you can use any pasta. We have shown it with pappardelle. If you are short on time and don't have 15 minutes to reduce the sauce, it can be thickened with 2 teaspoons of cornflour (cornstarch) mixed with 1 tablespoon of water. Stir until the mixture boils and thickens.

Spinach and ricotta cannelloni

SERVES 6 **PREPARATION TIME** 30 minutes (+ 10 minutes standing) **COOKING TIME** 1 hour 5 minutes

16 dried cannelloni tubes, about
    10 cm (4 inches) long x 2.5 cm
    (1 inch) wide
125 g (4 oz/1 cup) grated mozzarella
    cheese
60 g (2¼ oz/½ cup) coarsely grated
    parmesan cheese

TOMATO SAUCE
1 tablespoon olive oil
1 brown onion, finely chopped
1–2 garlic cloves, chopped
400 g (14 oz) tin chopped tomatoes
1 tablespoon tomato paste
    (concentrated purée)
1 teaspoon white sugar
2 tablespoons chopped basil

WHITE SAUCE
50 g (1¾ oz) butter
50 g (1¾ oz/⅓ cup) plain
    (all-purpose) flour
750 ml (26 fl oz/3 cups) milk
¼ teaspoon freshly grated nutmeg

FILLING
450 g (1 lb) English spinach, stems
    removed, chopped (trimmed
    weight 360 g/12¾ oz)
1 tablespoon olive oil
1 large onion, finely chopped
2–3 garlic cloves, finely chopped
350 g (12 oz) ricotta cheese
1 egg, lightly beaten
½ teaspoon freshly grated nutmeg

1 Preheat the oven to 180°C (350°F/ Gas 4). Grease an ovenproof dish, measuring about 20 x 26 x 6 cm (8 x 10½ x 2½ inches).

2 To make the tomato sauce, heat the oil in a large frying pan over medium heat. Add the onion and garlic and cook for 2–3 minutes. Add the tomatoes, tomato paste, sugar and 125 ml (4 fl oz/½ cup) water. Simmer for 20 minutes or until the mixture thickens slightly, then stir in the basil.

3 To make the white sauce, melt the butter in a saucepan. Add the flour and cook for 1 minute. Remove from the heat, gradually add the milk and whisk until smooth (*pic 1*). Return to the heat and stir until thick. Add the nutmeg and simmer for 3 minutes or until the sauce boils and thickens. Season with salt and freshly ground black pepper.

4 To make the filling, put the spinach and 100 ml (3½ fl oz) water in a large saucepan. Cover and cook for 3 minutes or until the spinach has wilted, then refresh under cold water. Squeeze out any excess moisture with your hands and chop finely (*pic 2*). Heat the oil in a small frying pan over medium heat. Add the onion and garlic and cook for 2 minutes or until soft. Transfer to a large bowl, add the ricotta, egg and nutmeg and combine with a fork. Stir through the spinach. Spoon into the cannelloni tubes.

5 Spread half of the white sauce onto the base of the dish, then drizzle over half of the tomato sauce. Arrange the filled cannelloni tubes evenly in a single layer (*pic 3*). Top with the remaining white sauce, then tomato sauce and sprinkle over the mozzarella and parmesan. Bake for 40 minutes or until cooked. Stand for 10 minutes before serving.

TIP Use a teaspoon to stuff the mixture into the tubes.

Tagliatelle bolognese

Perhaps the best-known and best-loved of all pasta sauces, bolognese is made with a meat-rich mixture of minced beef and pork plus pancetta. Long, slow cooking makes the sauce intensely flavoursome. Long pastas such as tagliatelle, spaghetti and linguine suit this sauce best.

SERVES 4–6 **PREPARATION TIME** 15 minutes **COOKING TIME** 2 hours 15 minutes

60 ml (2 fl oz/¼ cup) olive oil
1 large brown onion, finely chopped
2 garlic cloves, crushed
1 celery stalk, finely chopped
1 large carrot, finely chopped
¼ cup flat-leaf (Italian)
   parsley, chopped
500 g (1 lb 2 oz) minced (ground)
   beef
250 g (9 oz) minced (ground) pork
50 g (1¾ oz) sliced pancetta,
   finely chopped
2 x 400 g (14 oz) tins chopped
   tomatoes
50 g (1¾ oz) tomato paste
   (concentrated purée)
125 ml (4 fl oz/½ cup) red or
   white wine
250 ml (9 fl oz/1 cup) beef stock
500 g (1 lb 2 oz) dried tagliatelle or
   or 600 g (1 lb 5 oz) fresh tagliatelle
   (see pages 8–13)
shaved parmesan cheese, to serve

1   Heat the oil in a large frying pan. Add the onion and garlic, and cook over medium–low heat for 3 minutes or until soft. Add the celery, carrot and parsley (*pic 1*). Cook, stirring, for 3 minutes.

2   Add the beef and pork mince. Break up any lumps with a wooden spoon (*pic 2*). Cook, stirring, for 4–5 minutes or until the meat starts to brown.

3   Add the pancetta, tomato, tomato paste, wine and stock (*pic 3*). Season with salt and freshly ground black pepper. Simmer, partially covered, for 2 hours. Add a little stock or water if the sauce becomes too dry.

4   When the sauce is almost ready, cook the pasta in a large saucepan of boiling salted water, following the packet instructions, until al dente. Drain well.

5   Serve the pasta with the meat sauce and parmesan.

1

2

3

Spaghetti vongole

The brininess of the clams instantly transports you to a Mediterranean trattoria. Whether using fresh or tinned clams, this dish relies on simple flavours, so the quality of the clams is paramount. If using fresh clams, make sure they are completely purged of any grit as there is nothing more dissatisfying than biting into a sandy clam.

SERVES 4 **PREPARATION TIME** 25 minutes **COOKING TIME** 35 minutes

1 kg (2 lb 4 oz) live baby clams (vongole) or 750 g (1 lb 10 oz) tin clams in brine
1 tablespoon lemon juice
80 ml (2½ fl oz/⅓ cup) olive oil
3 garlic cloves, crushed
800 g (1 lb 12 oz) tin chopped tomatoes
250 g (9 oz) dried spaghetti or 600 g (1 lb 5 oz) fresh spaghetti (see pages 8–13)
⅓ cup chopped flat-leaf (Italian) parsley

1 If using fresh clams, clean thoroughly. Place in a large saucepan with the lemon juice. Cover the pan and shake over medium heat for 7–8 minutes or until the shells open, discarding any that don't open. Remove the clam meat from the shells and set aside. If using tinned clams, drain, rinse well and set aside.

2 Heat the oil in a large saucepan over low heat. Add the garlic and cook for 5 minutes. Add the tomatoes and stir to combine. Bring to the boil and simmer, covered, for 20 minutes. Season with freshly ground black pepper, add the clam meat and stir until heated through.

3 Meanwhile, cook the pasta in a large saucepan of boiling salted water, following the packet instructions, until al dente. Drain and return to the pan. Gently stir in the sauce and the parsley to combine.

TIP When buying clams from the fishmonger, ask if they have been purged (stored in aerated salt water to eliminate sand). If not, place the clams in a bowl and wash them under cold running water, then add 60 g (2¼ oz) salt to 2 litres (70 fl oz) water and stand for several hours in a cool place. This recreates their natural environment and they will breathe and filter the water, releasing any sand from within their shells.

Ricotta, spinach and lemon ravioli

This is a satisfying dish to prepare when you have time for the whole process of making pasta and ravioli. If you get another person involved, it will be quicker and more fun. Cook the ravioli that day or simply freeze it (see tip, page 15) so you can enjoy your efforts another day.

SERVES 4–6   **PREPARATION TIME** 45 minutes   **COOKING TIME** 15 minutes

350 g (12 oz) English spinach,
   trimmed and washed
150 g (5½ oz) ricotta cheese
25 g (1 oz) finely grated
   parmesan cheese
½ teaspoon finely grated
   lemon zest
1 quantity fresh pasta dough
   (see page 8)
1 egg, lightly beaten
80 g (2¾ oz) butter, chopped
⅔ cup sage leaves
shaved parmesan cheese, to serve

1   Cook the spinach in boiling salted water until just wilted. Drain and immerse in iced water to cool completely. Drain, squeeze out all the moisture (*pic 1*), finely chop (*pic 2*) and combine in a bowl with the ricotta, parmesan and lemon zest. Season with salt and freshly ground black pepper.

2   To prevent the dough from drying out, work in batches, using one-quarter of the dough at a time and leaving the rest covered with a clean cloth until needed. Roll out the pasta dough, following the step-by-step instructions on pages 10–11, to form sheets of pasta about 1 mm (1/32 inch) thick and about 14 cm (5½ inches) wide. Working with one sheet at a time, place 1 teaspoon of ricotta mixture on one of the pasta sheets, leaving about 4 cm (1½ inches) in between each mound (see page 14). Brush around the filling with some egg. Place another pasta sheet on top,

then press around the edge of each mound of filling to enclose it, taking care to expel any air.

3   Cut the ravioli into 6.5 cm (2½ inch) squares using a fluted pastry wheel if you have one, or a sharp knife. Place, so that they don't touch each other, on trays lined with lightly floured baking paper. Repeat with the remaining dough and filling.

4   Cook the pasta in a large saucepan of boiling salted water for 7 minutes or until al dente.

5   Meanwhile, melt the butter in a frying pan over high heat. When it starts to turn nut brown, add the sage and continue to cook for 1 minute or until the foam subsides and the butter is golden with light-brown flecks (*pic 3*). If you overcook and burn the butter, the flecks will be dark brown and it will taste bitter.

6   Drain the ravioli and combine in a large bowl with the butter and sage sauce. Gently toss to coat and season with salt and pepper. Serve with the parmesan.

1

2

3

TIP Avoid piling up the uncooked ravioli, as they will stick together. Place, without allowing them to touch one another, on trays lined with lightly floured baking paper.

Pastitsio

Pasta bakes such as this are very convenient, as the meat sauce can be made up to two days ahead, then the pasta and white sauce prepared just before you bake the dish. This is a good alternative to lasagne, and a simple yet hearty dish.

SERVES 6–8 **PREPARATION TIME** 30 minutes (+ 10 minutes standing) **COOKING TIME** 1 hour 50 minutes

250 g (9 oz) dried penne
2 eggs, lightly beaten
50 g (1¾ oz/½ cup) coarsely grated
   cheddar cheese
60 g (2¼ oz/½ cup) coarsely
   grated parmesan cheese
½ teaspoon freshly grated nutmeg

MEAT SAUCE
1 tablespoon olive oil
1 brown onion, finely chopped
2–3 garlic cloves, chopped
500 g (1 lb 2 oz) minced
   (ground) beef
400 g (14 oz) tin chopped tomatoes
50 g (1¾ oz/¼ cup) tomato paste
   (concentrated purée)
1 teaspoon dried oregano
125 ml (4 fl oz/½ cup) white wine
125 ml (4 fl oz/½ cup) beef stock
   or water
¼ cup flat-leaf (Italian) parsley,
   chopped

WHITE SAUCE
50 g (1¾ oz) butter
35 g (1¼ oz/¼ cup) plain
   (all-purpose) flour
750 ml (26 fl oz/3 cups) milk
1 egg, lightly beaten
¼ teaspoon freshly grated nutmeg
30 g (1 oz/¼ cup) finely
   grated parmesan cheese
30 g (1 oz/¼ cup) dry breadcrumbs

1 Preheat oven to 180°C (350°F/ Gas 4). Grease an ovenproof dish (23 x 30 x 5 cm/9 x 12 x 2 inches).

2 Cook pasta in a large saucepan of boiling salted water, following the packet instructions, until al dente. Cool under cold running water and drain. Stir through egg, cheeses and nutmeg and season with salt and pepper.

3 To make meat sauce, heat oil in a large frying pan. Add onion and garlic and cook over medium heat for 2–3 minutes or until soft. Add meat and cook, stirring, for 3–4 minutes or until meat changes colour.

4 Add tomatoes, tomato paste, oregano, wine and stock or water. Simmer for 45 minutes. Use a potato masher or fork to break up any lumps in meat (*pic 1*). Set aside.

5 To make white sauce, melt butter in a saucepan over low heat, add flour and cook for 1 minute. Remove from heat and gradually whisk in milk until smooth. Return to heat; stir until thick. Simmer for 3 minutes, then set aside. Allow to cool a little before whisking in egg and nutmeg. Pour 125 ml (4 fl oz/½ cup) of sauce into meat mixture (*pic 2*) and stir through parsley.

6 Spoon half of pasta mixture evenly into prepared dish. Spoon over meat sauce (*pic 3*), then remaining pasta mixture. Pour on white sauce; sprinkle with combined parmesan and breadcrumbs. Bake for 50 minutes — cover with foil if browning too much. Stand for 10 minutes before serving.

1

2

3

Weeknights

Risoni and spring vegetable soup with pesto

This soup makes a substantial first course or light meal. If you like, you could add some shredded poached chicken for the last 3–4 minutes of cooking, just to heat it through.

SERVES 4   **PREPARATION TIME** 10 minutes   **COOKING TIME** 35 minutes

80 ml (2½ fl oz/⅓ cup) olive oil
1 large red onion, finely chopped
3 celery stalks, finely chopped
2 garlic cloves, crushed
1 bunch asparagus, trimmed and
   cut into small pieces
125 g (4½ oz) young green beans,
   trimmed and cut into small pieces
100 g (3½ oz) sugar snap peas,
   trimmed and halved
80 g (2¾ oz/½ cup) fresh
   or frozen peas
1.25 litres (44 fl oz/5 cups)
   vegetable or chicken stock
180 g (6¼ oz/¾ cup) dried
   risoni
85 g (3 oz/⅓ cup) pesto
   (see page 33)

1 Heat the oil in a large saucepan over medium–low heat and gently cook the onion, celery and garlic until soft.

2 Divide the asparagus, beans, sugar snap peas and peas into two separate bowls. Add half of the vegetables to the saucepan and cook for 3–4 minutes.

3 Pour in the stock (*pic 1*), bring to the boil and simmer, covered, for about 20 minutes.

4 Blend the vegetables and stock with a stick blender (*pic 2*). Add the pasta and cook, uncovered, for about 7 minutes (or 3 minutes less than the recommended cooking time on the packet instructions).

5 Add the remaining vegetables (*pic 3*), cook for 3–4 minutes, then season with salt and freshly ground black pepper.

6 Divide among warmed bowls and serve topped with the pesto.

1

2

3

TIP Risoni, also known as orzo, is a small, rice-shaped pasta. It is often used in soups and salads.

Calabrian spaghetti

Calabria in the south of Italy is renowned for the use of chilli in their cooking. Calabrian cuisine has a fiery heat, which is relatively uncommon for dishes in other parts of Italy. Feel free to add more or less chillies as you like and experiment with different types of hot chillies too.

SERVES 4   **PREPARATION TIME** 10 minutes   **COOKING TIME** 10 minutes

500 g (1 lb 2 oz) dried spaghetti or
   600 g (1 lb 5 oz) fresh spaghetti
   (see pages 8–13)
80 ml (2½ fl oz/⅓ cup) olive oil
3 garlic cloves, crushed
50 g (1¾ oz) anchovies,
   finely chopped, plus extra, to serve
1 teaspoon thinly sliced red chillies,
   plus extra, to serve (optional)
¼ cup chopped flat-leaf (Italian)
   parsley
grated parmesan cheese, to serve

1   Cook the pasta in a large saucepan of boiling salted water, following the packet instructions, until al dente. Drain and return to the pan.

2   Meanwhile, heat the oil in a small saucepan over low heat. Add the garlic, anchovy and chilli and cook for 5 minutes, being careful not to brown the garlic too much or it will be bitter. Add the parsley and cook for 3 minutes. Season with salt and freshly ground black pepper.

3   Add the sauce to the pasta and toss through until thoroughly coated. Serve immediately, garnished with the cheese.

Roast tomato, bocconcini and basil spaghetti

Heirloom tomatoes, both regular and miniature varieties, are increasingly available at farmers' markets and even supermarkets. Their varied colours and shapes make for an attractive presentation, but if you can't find them, substitute cherry or grape tomatoes (or a mixture).

SERVES 4–6   **PREPARATION TIME** 10 minutes   **COOKING TIME** 45 minutes

800 g (1 lb 12 oz) mixed small heirloom tomatoes
125 ml (4 fl oz/½ cup) extra virgin olive oil, plus extra, to serve
1 tablespoon red wine vinegar
3 teaspoons caster (superfine) sugar
400 g (14 oz) dried spaghetti or 600 g (1 lb 5 oz) fresh spaghetti (see pages 8–13)
250 g (9 oz) bocconcini (fresh baby mozzarella cheese), torn into rough pieces
½ cup basil leaves, torn

1   Preheat the oven to 180°C (350°F/ Gas 4). Cut the smaller tomatoes in half lengthways and larger tomatoes into quarters. Place the tomato in a roasting tray in a single layer, drizzle with 2 tablespoons of the oil and the vinegar, then sprinkle with the sugar and season with salt and pepper (*pic 1*). Roast the tomatoes for 40 minutes or until light golden (*pic 2*).

2   Cook the pasta in a large saucepan of boiling salted water, following the packet instructions, until al dente. Drain and return the pasta to the pan. Add the remaining oil, the bocconcini, basil, roast tomatoes and pan juices (*pic 3*) and toss over low heat to combine well.

3   Divide among warmed bowls and serve immediately.

1

2

3

Chicken and spinach orzo soup

Nearly every culture has a nourishing, healthy chicken soup to warm the soul and this is the Greek version. It's spiked with vitamin-C rich lemon juice to ward off colds, making it the perfect bowl on a wintery night. Use a good-quality chicken stock, or, even better, make your own from a whole chicken, then shred the meat into the soup.

SERVES 4　**PREPARATION TIME** 10 minutes　**COOKING TIME** 30 minutes

1 tablespoon olive oil
1 leek, trimmed and cut into quarters
　lengthways, then rinsed well
　and thinly sliced
2 garlic cloves, crushed
1 teaspoon ground cumin
1.5 litres (52 fl oz/6 cups)
　chicken stock
2 skinless chicken breast fillets,
　about 500 g (1 lb 2 oz) in total
200 g (7 oz/1 cup) dried orzo
150 g (5½ oz/3 cups) baby spinach
　leaves, roughly chopped
1 tablespoon chopped dill
2 teaspoons lemon juice

1　Heat the oil in a large saucepan over low heat. Add the leek and cook for 8–10 minutes or until soft. Add the garlic and cumin and cook for 1 minute.

2　Pour in the stock, increase the heat to high and bring to the boil. Reduce the heat to low, add the chicken, then cover and simmer for 8 minutes. Remove the chicken, reserving the liquid (keep it covered over low heat to keep it hot). When the chicken is cool enough to handle, use your fingers to shred it finely.

3　Stir the pasta into the simmering stock and simmer for 12 minutes or until al dente.

4　Return the chicken to the pan and add the spinach and dill. Simmer for 2 minutes or until the spinach has wilted. Stir in the lemon juice, season with salt and freshly ground black pepper and serve.

TIP Orzo, also known as risoni, is a small, rice-shaped pasta. It is often used in soups and salads.

Pesto chicken pasta

This summery pasta salad is ideal for packing on a picnic, or into school or office lunchboxes. You can add chargrilled capsicum (pepper) or marinated artichokes, or roast the cherry tomatoes for an added depth of flavour.

SERVES 4 **PREPARATION TIME** 15 minutes **COOKING TIME** 15 minutes

250 g (9 oz) dried penne or fusilli
1 small barbecued chicken
125 g (4½ oz/1 cup) walnuts
4 bacon rashers
250 g (9 oz) cherry tomatoes, halved
60 g (2¼ oz) pitted and sliced olives
125 g (4½ oz/½ cup) pesto (see page 33)
30 g (1 oz/½ cup) finely shredded basil leaves

1 Cook the pasta in a large saucepan of boiling salted water, following the packet instructions, until al dente. Drain well.

2 Meanwhile, discard the skin of the chicken. Remove the meat from the chicken, cut or shred it into bite-sized pieces and put in a large bowl.

3 Toast the walnuts for 2–3 minutes under a hot grill (broiler), allow to cool and then chop roughly.

4 Remove the rind from the bacon and grill (broil) for 3–4 minutes or until crisp. Allow to cool and then roughly chop. Add the bacon, nuts, tomato and olives to the chicken.

5 Add the pasta to the chicken mixture, along with the pesto and basil. Toss until thoroughly mixed. Serve at room temperature.

TIP You probably won't need to add salt as the olives and bacon are already quite salty.

Farfalle with tuna, mushrooms and cream

This quick and easy dish is incredibly versatile. You can replace the tinned tuna with tinned salmon (drained and flaked) and use dill instead of parsley, or try tinned mussels (drained) and swap the parsley for sprigs of chervil.

SERVES 4 **PREPARATION TIME** 10 minutes **COOKING TIME** 15 minutes

60 g (2¼ oz) butter
1 tablespoon olive oil
1 onion, chopped
1 garlic clove, crushed
125 g (4½ oz) button
    mushrooms, sliced
250 ml (9 fl oz/1 cup) thin
    (pouring) cream
425 g (15 oz) tin tuna in brine,
    drained and flaked
1 tablespoon lemon juice
1 tablespoon chopped flat-leaf
    (Italian) parsley
500 g (1 lb 2 oz) dried farfalle

1 Heat the butter and oil in a large frying pan over low heat. Add the onion and garlic and stir for 3–5 minutes or until the onion is soft. Add the mushrooms and cook for 2 minutes. Pour in the cream, bring to the boil, then reduce the heat and simmer until the sauce begins to thicken. Add the tuna, lemon juice and parsley and stir until heated through. Season with salt and freshly ground black pepper.

2 Meanwhile, cook the pasta in a large saucepan of boiling salted water, following the packet instructions, until al dente. Drain and return to the pan. Add the sauce to the pasta and toss to combine.

TIP Don't wash the mushrooms, as the water penetrates the delicate flesh and makes them soggy. Instead, wipe them gently with a damp cloth or paper towel.

Spaghetti Siciliana

Bursting with barely cooked vegetables, this pasta is a quick and nutritious option. If you want a vegetarian version, simply omit the anchovies and add some dried chilli flakes instead. Fettuccine and bucatini could also work well in this dish if you want a change from spaghetti.

SERVES 4 **PREPARATION TIME** 15 minutes **COOKING TIME** 40 minutes

2 ripe tomatoes
60 ml (2 fl oz/¼ cup) olive oil
1 brown onion, finely chopped
2–3 garlic cloves, finely chopped
2 baby eggplants (aubergines), sliced
1 yellow capsicum (pepper), cut into thin strips
1 green capsicum (pepper), cut into thin strips
1 zucchini (courgette), sliced
400 g (14 oz) tin chopped tomatoes
1 tablespoon capers, rinsed and chopped
4–5 anchovies, drained and chopped
40 g (1½ oz/⅓ cup) black olives, pitted and sliced
500 g (1 lb 2 oz) dried spaghetti or 600 g (1 lb 5 oz) fresh spaghetti (see pages 8–13)
basil leaves, torn, to garnish
grated parmesan cheese, to serve

1 Score a cross in the base of each tomato. Soak the tomatoes in boiling water for 1–2 minutes, drain and plunge into cold water briefly. Peel back the skin from the cross. Halve, remove the seeds and chop the flesh.

2 Heat the oil in a large frying pan over medium heat. Add the onion, garlic and eggplant and cook for 5 minutes or until the onion and eggplant are soft. Add the capsicum and zucchini (*pic 1*) and cook for 3 minutes.

3 Add the tinned and fresh tomatoes (*pic 2*) and simmer for 20 minutes. Add the capers, anchovies and olives and simmer for 10 minutes or until the sauce thickens slightly.

4 Meanwhile, cook the pasta in a large saucepan of boiling salted water, following the packet instructions, until al dente (*pic 3*). Drain and return to the pan.

5 Toss the sauce through the pasta, garnish with the basil and serve with the cheese.

1

2

3

TIP Use the best-quality olives you can find. Kalamata are the obvious choice, but also look out for manzanilla, a round and fleshy Spanish variety available at delis and gourmet food stores.

Conchiglie with broccolini

Conchiglie means seashell in Italian. This shell pasta is ideal for scooping up sauces. Its little pockets pick up the sauce so every bite is full of flavour. If using broccoli, don't throw away the stem — it's just as delicious as the florets. Simply slice it thinly and cook for 2 minutes in the pan of boiling water until tender.

SERVES 4　**PREPARATION TIME** 10 minutes　**COOKING TIME** 10 minutes

500 g (1 lb 2 oz) dried conchiglie
450 g (1 lb) broccolini or broccoli
1 tablespoon olive oil
1 onion, chopped
1 garlic clove, crushed
3 anchovies, chopped
310 ml (10¾ fl oz/1¼ cups) thin (pouring) cream
50 g (1¾ oz/½ cup) shredded parmesan cheese, to serve

1　Cook the pasta in a large saucepan of boiling salted water, following the packet instructions, until al dente. Drain and return to the pan.

2　Meanwhile, cut the broccolini into short lengths and cook in a saucepan of boiling water for 1 minute. Drain, plunge into cold water and drain again. Set aside.

3　Heat the oil in a frying pan over low heat. Add the onion, garlic and anchovies and cook, stirring, for 3 minutes.

4　Add the cream to the pan and, stirring constantly, bring to the boil. Reduce the heat and simmer for 2 minutes. Add the broccolini and cook for 1 minute. Season with salt and freshly ground black pepper. Toss the sauce through the pasta until well combined and serve sprinkled with the cheese.

Mixed mushroom pasta

The mushrooms used here can vary depending on what is available — for example, you could add pine mushrooms when in season. Fresh pasta is the ideal partner for rich creamy sauces; a lightweight dried pasta would also work. If you like, use chives or flat-leaf (Italian) parsley instead of tarragon.

SERVES 4 **PREPARATION TIME** 15 minutes **COOKING TIME** 15 minutes

5 g (⅛ oz) dried mushrooms, broken roughly
80 ml (2½ fl oz/⅓ cup) olive oil
2 French shallots, chopped
750 g (1 lb 10 oz) mixed fresh mushrooms, such as portobello, oyster, flat, button and Swiss brown mushrooms, sliced 1 cm (½ inch) thick
3 garlic cloves, chopped
300 ml (10½ fl oz) thin (pouring) cream
¼ cup chopped tarragon
400 g (14 oz) fresh fettuccine (see pages 8–13)

1 Place the dried mushrooms in a small bowl, pour 2 tablespoons boiling water over them and allow to stand for 15 minutes (*pic 1*). Strain, reserving the soaking liquid.

2 Heat the oil in a large, deep frying pan over low heat, add the shallots and cook over low heat for about 2 minutes or until soft. Increase the heat to medium–high, add the fresh mushrooms and cook, stirring occasionally, for about 5 minutes or until tender (*pic 2*).

3 Add the garlic and rehydrated dried mushrooms and stir over medium heat for 1 minute. Stir in the cream and soaking liquid, bring to the boil, then simmer over medium heat for about 5 minutes or until the cream has thickened slightly. Stir in the tarragon (*pic 3*) and season with salt and freshly ground black pepper.

4 Meanwhile, cook the pasta in a large saucepan of boiling salted water until al dente. Drain and return to the pan. Toss the pasta with half the mushroom sauce and serve topped with the remaining mushroom sauce.

1

2

3

TIP Don't wash the mushrooms, as the water penetrates the delicate flesh and makes them soggy. Instead, wipe them gently with a damp cloth or paper towel.

Chicken pasta with basil and lemon

Asparagus is at its most flavoursome during springtime. This is when thin asparagus, which is young and tender, is readily available. You can also use larger asparagus, but make sure to remove the tough bases first. To do this, gently bend the spear and it will break at the natural division between the woody base and the tender upper part of the stem.

SERVES 4 **PREPARATION TIME** 15 minutes **COOKING TIME** 20 minutes

600 g (1 lb 5 oz) skinless chicken
    breast fillets, trimmed
2 tablespoons olive oil
400 g (14 oz) dried spaghetti or
    600 g (1 lb 5 oz) fresh spaghetti
    (see pages 8–13)
200 g (7 oz) thin asparagus spears,
    trimmed and halved
2 leeks, white part only, sliced
245 g (9 oz/1 cup) sour cream
80 ml (2½ fl oz/⅓ cup) lemon juice
finely grated zest of 1 lemon
1 cup small basil leaves

1 Brush the chicken with half the oil and season with salt and freshly ground black pepper. Heat a non-stick frying pan over medium heat. Cook the chicken for 5 minutes each side or until golden and just cooked through. Remove from the pan, set aside to cool slightly and then use two forks to coarsely shred the chicken (*pic 1*).

2 Cook the pasta in a large saucepan of boiling salted water, following the packet instructions, until al dente. Add the asparagus for the final 2 minutes of cooking (*pic 2*). It should be bright green and tender when the pasta is ready. Drain, reserving a little of the cooking liquid.

3 Meanwhile, heat the remaining oil in a large saucepan over medium–low heat. Add the leeks and cook, stirring occasionally, for 6–8 minutes or until softened and light golden (*pic 3*). Add the sour cream and lemon juice and stir to combine. Add the shredded chicken and cook for 1 minute to heat through. Add the lemon zest and drained pasta and asparagus, and toss to coat. Add a little of the reserved cooking liquid if the sauce is too thick. Taste and adjust the seasoning, then stir through the basil and serve.

1

2

3

Sun-dried tomato sauce on tagliatelle

Sun-dried tomatoes add an intensity of flavour to this sauce. If you want a quick meal, just use dried tagliatelle, but fresh pasta will soak up this delicious sauce more and add a wonderful bite. If you have some pasta already made and frozen in the freezer, this is the perfect dish to use it in or buy fresh pasta in the refrigerated section at supermarkerts.

SERVES 4   **PREPARATION TIME** 10 minutes   **COOKING TIME** 20 minutes

600 g (1 lb 5 oz) fresh tagliatelle
   (see pages 8–13) or 500 g
   (1 lb 2 oz) dried tagliatelle
2 tablespoons olive oil
1 onion, chopped
80 g (2¾ oz/½ cup) thinly sliced
   sun-dried (sun-blushed) tomatoes
2 garlic cloves, crushed
400 g (14 oz) tin chopped
   tomatoes
125 g (4½ oz/1 cup) pitted
   black olives
20 g (¾ oz/⅓ cup) chopped basil
shaved parmesan cheese, to serve

1   Cook the pasta in a large saucepan of boiling salted water, following the packet instructions, until al dente. Drain and return to the pan.

2   Meanwhile, heat the oil in a large frying pan over medium heat. Add the onion and cook for 3 minutes, stirring occasionally, until soft. Add the sun-dried tomato and garlic and cook for another minute.

3   Add the tomatoes, olives and basil to the onion mixture and season with freshly ground black pepper. Bring to the boil, reduce the heat, and simmer for 10 minutes.

4   Add the sauce to the hot pasta and gently toss through. Serve immediately, topped with the cheese.

TIP Sun-dried (sun-blushed) tomatoes are available dry or loosely packed, or in jars with olive or canola oil. The tomatoes in oil need only to be drained, but the dry tomatoes must be soaked in boiling water for 5 minutes to rehydrate and soften them.

Rigatoni with sausage and parmesan

Italian pork sausages are typically aromatic with herbs such as fennel, thyme and/or parsley. Buy the best-quality ones you can find, preferably from a butcher. You can replace the sausages with salami or another cured meat if you prefer.

SERVES 4   **PREPARATION TIME** 15 minutes   **COOKING TIME** 20 minutes

2 tablespoons olive oil

1 onion, sliced

1 garlic clove, crushed

500 g (1 lb 2 oz) Italian pork sausage, thickly sliced on the diagonal

60 g (2¼ oz) button mushrooms, sliced

125 ml (4 fl oz/½ cup) dry white wine

500 g (1 lb 2 oz) dried rigatoni

250 ml (9 fl oz/1 cup) pouring (whipping) cream

2 eggs

50 g (1¾ oz/½ cup) shredded parmesan cheese

2 tablespoons chopped flat-leaf (Italian) parsley

1   Heat the oil in a large frying pan over low heat. Add the onion and garlic and stir over low heat until the onion is tender. Add the sausage and mushroom and cook until the sausage is cooked through. Stir in the wine and bring to the boil. Reduce the heat and simmer until the liquid is reduced by half.

2   Meanwhile, cook the pasta in a large saucepan of boiling salted water, following the packet instructions, until al dente. Drain and return to the pan.

3   In a large jug, whisk together the cream, eggs, half the cheese, the parsley and season with salt and freshly ground black pepper. Add to the pasta with the sausage mixture and toss. Serve sprinkled with the remaining cheese.

TIP You can freeze leftover wine for use in recipes such as this one.

Orecchiette with broccoli, chillies and anchovies

This is a classic dish, and while it's quick and simple, it has bold flavour. Broccolini can be used instead of broccoli and you can add more or less chilli to taste. For a variation, substitute chopped pancetta for the anchovies and use a different type of pasta, such as a medium-sized shell pasta.

SERVES 4 **PREPARATION TIME** 10 minutes **COOKING TIME** 15 minutes

400 g (14 oz) dried orecchiette

300 g (10½ oz) trimmed broccoli (about 450 g/1 lb untrimmed), cut into 2.5 cm (1 inch) florets

60 ml (2 fl oz/¼ cup) extra virgin olive oil

30 g (1 oz) coarsely chopped anchovies

2 small red chillies, sliced diagonally

2 garlic cloves, thinly sliced

¼ cup flat-leaf (Italian) parsley leaves, roughly chopped

35 g (1¼ oz/⅓ cup) finely grated pecorino cheese, to serve

1 Cook the pasta in a large saucepan of boiling salted water until it is 5 minutes away from being completely cooked. Add the broccoli (*pic 1*) and continue cooking for 5 minutes or until the pasta is al dente. Drain and return to the pan.

2 Heat the oil in a large non-stick frying pan over low heat, add the anchovies and chilli and stir for about 2 minutes or until the anchovies are softened. Add the garlic and stir for about 1 minute or until golden (*pic 2*). Take care — you don't want to overcook the garlic, as it will become bitter.

3 Add the drained pasta mixture to the pan and toss over low heat (*pic 3*), adding a little more oil if necessary. Stir in the parsley.

4 Serve immediately, sprinkled with the cheese.

TIP The anchovies are a big flavour in this dish; reduce the quantity of them if you like.

Gorgonzola and toasted walnuts on linguine

Gorgonzola and walnuts come together in this simple yet satisfying dish. Don't skip toasting the walnuts as this brings out the creaminess of the nut and mellows any bitter flavours. You can use any strong-flavoured blue cheese, just make sure it is soft and creamy.

SERVES 4 **PREPARATION TIME** 15 minutes **COOKING TIME** 15 minutes

75 g (2½ oz/¾ cup) walnut halves
500 g (1 lb 2 oz) dried linguine or
    600 g (1 lb 5 oz) fresh linguine
    (see pages 8–13)
70 g (2½ oz) butter, chopped
150 g (5½ oz) gorgonzola
    cheese, crumbled
2 tablespoons pouring
    (whipping) cream
155 g (5½ oz/1 cup) shelled fresh
    peas (about 450 g/1 lb in the pod)

1 Preheat the oven to 180°C (350°F/ Gas 4). Place the walnuts on a baking tray in a single layer and bake for about 5 minutes or until lightly toasted. Cool.

2 Cook the pasta in a large saucepan of boiling salted water, following the packet instructions, until al dente. Drain and return to the pan.

3 Meanwhile, melt the butter in a small saucepan over low heat and add the gorgonzola, cream and peas. Stir gently for 5 minutes or until the sauce has thickened. Season with salt and freshly ground black pepper. Add the sauce and walnuts to the pasta and toss until well combined. Serve immediately, sprinkled with pepper.

TIP To get 155 g (5½ oz/1 cup) shelled fresh peas, you will need about 450 g (1 lb) of peas in the pod.

Chicken and spinach lasagne

This twist on the classic lasagne will quickly become a family favourite. The addition of sweet English spinach is a lovely contrast to the rich creamy cheese sauce. Try using silverbeet (Swiss chard) or Tuscan black kale (cavolo nero) instead of the spinach for a more robust flavour.

SERVES 8 **PREPARATION TIME** 30 minutes **COOKING TIME** 1 hour 15 minutes

500 g (1 lb 2 oz) English spinach
1 tablespoon olive oil
1 kg (2 lb 4 oz) minced
  (ground) chicken
1 garlic clove, crushed
3 bacon rashers, chopped
425 g (15 oz) tin chopped tomatoes
125 g (4$\frac{1}{2}$ oz/$\frac{1}{2}$ cup) tomato paste
  (concentrated purée)
125 ml (4 fl oz/$\frac{1}{2}$ cup) tomato
  passata (puréed tomatoes)
125 ml (4 fl oz/$\frac{1}{2}$ cup) chicken stock
60 g (2$\frac{1}{4}$ oz) butter
50 g (1$\frac{3}{4}$ oz/$\frac{1}{3}$ cup) plain
  (all-purpose) flour
625 ml (21$\frac{1}{2}$ fl oz/2$\frac{1}{2}$ cups) milk
12 instant lasagne sheets
250 g (9 oz/2 cups) coarsely grated
  cheddar cheese

1 Preheat the oven to 180°C (350°F/Gas 4). Remove and discard the stalks from the spinach. Plunge the leaves into a saucepan of boiling water for 2 minutes or until tender. Remove, plunge immediately into a bowl of iced water and then drain.

2 Heat the oil in a heavy-based frying pan over medium heat. Add the chicken, garlic and bacon and cook for 5 minutes or until browned. Stir in the tomatoes, tomato paste, passata and stock and bring to the boil. Reduce the heat and simmer, partially covered, for 10 minutes or until the sauce is slightly thickened. Season with salt and freshly ground pepper.

3 Meanwhile, melt the butter in a medium saucepan over low heat, add the flour and stir for 1 minute or until the mixture is lightly golden and smooth. Remove from the heat and gradually stir in the milk. Return to medium heat and stir constantly for 4 minutes or until the sauce boils and thickens. Remove from the heat and stir in half the cheese.

4 To assemble the lasagne, brush a 3 litre (105 fl oz) roasting tray or ovenproof dish with melted butter or oil. Spread one-third of the chicken mixture over the base. Top with 4 sheets of lasagne. Spread with one third of the cheese sauce, then another layer of the chicken mixture. Top with all of the spinach, another layer of lasagne, another layer of cheese sauce and the remaining chicken. Layer on the remaining lasagne and the remaining cheese sauce. Sprinkle over the remaining cheese to finish. Bake for 1 hour or until nicely golden on top. Remove from the oven and stand for 10 minutes before serving.

TIP You can replace the dried lasagne sheets with homemade ones or fresh ones from the supermarket. You need to blanch fresh lasagne sheets in boiling salted water until al dente, then drain well, before layering with the fillings and cheese sauce.

Tuscan warm pasta salad

The secret to making throw-it-together dishes, such as this pasta salad, taste great is to stock up your pantry with good-quality jarred ingredients. Olives, sun-dried tomatoes and marinated artichokes impart big, bold flavours and all that is needed is some rocket for freshness.

SERVES 4   **PREPARATION TIME** 15 minutes   **COOKING TIME** 10 minutes

500 g (1 lb 2 oz) dried rigatoni
80 ml (2½ fl oz/⅓ cup) olive oil
1 garlic clove, crushed
1 tablespoon balsamic vinegar
400 g (14 oz) marinated artichoke
   hearts, drained and quartered
8 thin prosciutto slices, chopped
80 g (2¾ oz/½ cup) sun-dried
   (sun-blushed) tomatoes in oil,
   drained and thinly sliced
15 g (½ oz/¼ cup) basil, shredded
70 g (2½ oz) rocket (arugula)
   leaves, washed and drained well
40 g (1½ oz/¼ cup) pine nuts,
   toasted
45 g (1½ oz/¼ cup) small black
   olives

1   Cook the pasta in a large saucepan of boiling salted water, following the packet instructions, until al dente. Drain and transfer to a bowl.

2   Meanwhile, whisk together the oil, garlic and balsamic vinegar. Toss the dressing through the hot pasta. Allow the pasta to cool slightly.

3   Add the artichoke, prosciutto, sun-dried tomato, basil, rocket, pine nuts and olives to the pasta. Toss together until well combined. Season with freshly ground black pepper.

TIPS To toast the pine nuts, cook in a dry frying pan over medium heat, shaking the pan occasionally, for 1–2 minutes or until lightly golden.
   You probably won't need to add salt as the olives and proscuitto are already quite salty.

Pasta with tuna, celery, lemon, basil and capers

A classic Mediterranean marriage of flavours. The capers add an important element to the dish — the salted small capers are the best ones to use, rather than those preserved in brine. If fresh tuna is not available, you could use kingfish or tinned tuna.

SERVES 4   **PREPARATION TIME** 25 minutes   **COOKING TIME** 20 minutes

125 ml (4 fl oz/½ cup) extra
    virgin olive oil
1 red onion, finely chopped
3 garlic cloves, thinly sliced
3 celery stalks, finely chopped
400 g (14 oz) dried short pasta
3 teaspoons finely grated
    lemon zest
60–80 ml (2–2½ fl oz/¼–⅓ cup)
    freshly squeezed lemon juice,
    or to taste
185 ml (6 fl oz/¾ cup) chicken stock
50 g (1¾ oz/¼ cup) baby capers,
    rinsed and drained
½ cup basil leaves
450 g (1 lb) tuna steaks, blood line
    trimmed, cut into small cubes
½ cup flat-leaf (Italian) parsley

1 Heat the oil in a large frying pan over medium–low heat, add the onion, garlic and celery and cook, stirring often, for 10 minutes or until the vegetables have softened (*pic 1*).

2 Meanwhile, cook the pasta in a large saucepan of boiling salted water, following the packet instructions, until al dente. Drain well and return to the pan.

3 Add the lemon zest and juice, stock and capers to the onion mixture. Tear the basil into the pan (*pic 2*), then season with salt, freshly ground black pepper and extra lemon juice. Add the tuna and toss over medium heat for 2–3 minutes (*pic 3*) or until heated through and the tuna has changed colour. Add to the pasta along with the parsley, toss to combine, then divide among warmed bowls and serve immediately.

1

2

3

TIP Use 2 x 185 g (6½ oz) tins of tuna in oil instead of fresh tuna. Drain, break into large chunks and heat very gently in the sauce.

Spaghetti tomato salad

This no-fuss dish contains the holy trinity of Italian flavours: tomato, basil and extra virgin olive oil. Black olives and balsamic vinegar are tossed in, too, to amp up the flavour. This dish will taste best in summer when tomatoes are at their best. Pick the juiciest, sweetest tomatoes you can find — be guided by what looks best at the market or greengrocer. We've used cherry tomatoes but look out for mini roma (plum), grape, oxheart (beefsteak) and heirloom varieties. If using larger tomatoes, simply cut down to size.

SERVES 4   **PREPARATION TIME** 10 minutes (+ 15 minutes standing)   **COOKING TIME** 10 minutes

500 g (1 lb 2 oz) dried spaghetti or bucatini 600 g (1 lb 5 oz) fresh long pasta (see pages 8–13)

50 g (1¾ oz/1 cup, firmly packed) basil leaves, shredded

250 g (9 oz) cherry tomatoes, halved

1 garlic clove, crushed

75 g (2¾ oz/½ cup) chopped pitted black olives

60 ml (2 fl oz/¼ cup) extra virgin olive oil

1 tablespoon balsamic vinegar

50 g (1¾ oz/½ cup) shredded parmesan cheese

1   Cook the pasta in a large saucepan of boiling salted water, following the packet instructions, until al dente. Drain, rinse under cold water and drain again. Set aside.

2   Combine the basil, tomato, garlic, olives, oil and vinegar in a salad bowl. Set aside for about 15 minutes. Mix in the drained pasta.

3   Add the cheese and season with freshly ground black pepper. Toss well and serve immediately.

TIPS Make sure you allow time for the pasta to soak up the dressing and for the flavours to meld.

You probably won't need to add salt as the olives are already quite salty.

Tortellini with mushroom sauce

If making your own tortellini, you can be as creative as you like as to the type of filling. Try spinach and ricotta; minced (ground) pork with saffron; minced chicken with pine nut; or leek and bacon. There are also many types of fresh tortellini readily available at the supermarket, so experiment and find one you and your family like.

SERVES 4   **PREPARATION TIME** 10 minutes   **COOKING TIME** 10 minutes

800 g (1 lb 12 oz) fresh tortellini
  (see pages 8–11 and 15)
90 g (3¼ oz) butter
280 g (10 oz) button mushrooms,
  sliced
1 large garlic clove, crushed
450 ml (16 fl oz) pouring
  (whipping) cream
1 lemon, zest finely grated
large pinch of freshly grated nutmeg
50 g (1¾ oz/½ cup) finely grated
  parmesan cheese, plus extra
  to serve
flat-leaf (Italian) parsley leaves,
  to garnish

1 Cook the pasta in a large saucepan of boiling salted water, following the packet instructions, until al dente. Drain, return to the pan and keep warm.

2 Meanwhile, melt the butter in a saucepan over medium heat and cook the mushrooms for 2 minutes. Add the garlic, cream, lemon zest, nutmeg and freshly ground black pepper. Stir over low heat for 1–2 minutes. Stir in the cheese and cook gently for 3 minutes.

3 Add the sauce to the pasta and stir gently to combine. Spoon into serving dishes, sprinkle with pepper and garnish with the parsley and extra cheese.

TIP Don't wash the mushrooms, as the water penetrates the delicate flesh and makes them soggy. Instead, wipe them gently with a damp cloth or paper towel.

Fettuccine with chicken and mushroom sauce

It's a good idea to use a good-quality white wine in this sauce — one that you're happy to drink. This sauce is quite simple so the aromatics of the wine will really carry through. If you don't have a bottle open, you could use dry vermouth, dry sherry or even marsala.

SERVES 4   **PREPARATION TIME** 20 minutes   **COOKING TIME** 20 minutes

500 g (1 lb 2 oz) dried fettuccine or
  or 600 g (1 lb 5 oz) fresh
  fettuccine (see pages 8–13)
1 tablespoon olive oil
30 g (1 oz) butter
2 large skinless chicken breast
  fillets, trimmed
2 bacon rashers, cut into long
  thin strips
2 garlic cloves, crushed
250 g (9 oz) button mushrooms,
  sliced
80 ml (2½ fl oz/⅓ cup) dry white
  wine
170 ml (5½ fl oz) thin
  (pouring) cream
4 spring onions (scallions), chopped
1 tablespoon plain (all-purpose)
  flour
shredded parmesan cheese, to serve

1   Cook the pasta in a large saucepan of boiling salted water, following the packet instructions, until al dente. Drain and return to the pan.

2   Meanwhile, heat the oil and butter in a heavy-based frying pan over medium heat, add the chicken and cook for 3 minutes or until browned. Add the bacon, garlic and mushrooms and cook for 2 minutes, stirring occasionally.

3   Add the wine and cook until the liquid has reduced by half. Add the cream and spring onion and bring to the boil. Blend the flour with 2 tablespoons of water until smooth, add to the pan and stir until the mixture boils and thickens. Reduce the heat and simmer for 2 minutes. Season with salt and freshly ground black pepper.

4   Add the sauce to the pasta and stir over low heat until combined. Sprinkle with the cheese to serve.

Pasta salad with roast vegetables

When making pasta for salad, toss it in a little oil once it's cooked. This will prevent the pasta from sticking together. You could replace the farfalle here with penne, fusilli or small conchiglie.

SERVES 6   **PREPARATION TIME** 15 minutes (+ 30 minutes cooling)   **COOKING TIME** 25 minutes

250 g (9 oz) dried farfalle
125 ml (4 fl oz/½ cup) extra virgin
   olive oil
1 large red onion, cut into 1 cm
   (½ inch) wedges
1 large zucchini (courgette), cut into
   2 cm (¾ inch) pieces
1 small eggplant (aubergine),
   cut into 2 cm (¾ inch) pieces
1 red capsicum (pepper), seeded
   and cut into 2 cm (¾ inch) pieces
1 yellow capsicum (pepper), seeded
   and cut into 2 cm (¾ inch) pieces
6 garlic cloves, unpeeled
250 g (9 oz) grape tomatoes
150 g (5 oz/1 cup) pitted kalamata
   olives, roughly chopped
2 tablespoons roughly chopped
   flat-leaf (Italian) parsley
2 tablespoons torn basil
2 tablespoons pine nuts, toasted

DRESSING
2 tablespoons extra virgin olive oil
1 tablespoon red wine vinegar

1   Preheat the oven to 200°C (400°F/ Gas 6). Cook the pasta in a large saucepan of boiling salted water, following the packet instructions, until al dente. Drain well. Toss with 1 tablespoon of the oil in a bowl and set aside to cool (*pic 1*).

2   Toss the onion, zucchini, eggplant, capsicum and garlic in 80 ml (2½ fl oz/ ⅓ cup) of the oil. Tip the mixture into one large or two smaller baking trays (*pic 2*). Put the tomatoes in a third baking tray, toss with the remaining oil and roast for 25–30 minutes or until golden and tender, tossing the vegetables halfway through the cooking time. Remove from the oven and allow to cool a little.

3   Remove the flesh from the roast garlic (*pic 3*).

4   Combine the ingredients for the dressing.

5   Transfer the roast vegetables to a large bowl and stir through the garlic and any juices and oil left in the baking trays. Add the dressing and stir through the pasta, olives and parsley. Set aside for 30 minutes for the flavours to develop. Add the basil, toss again, then sprinkle with the pine nuts. Serve at room temperature.

1

2

3

TIPS To toast the pine nuts, cook in a dry frying pan over medium heat, shaking the pan occasionally, for 1–2 minutes or until lightly golden.
   You probably won't need to add salt as the olives are already quite salty.

Fettuccine primavera

This classic pasta dish is filled with the seasonal vegetables of spring (primavera means spring in Italian) — think vibrant, grassy asparagus, nutty broad beans and sweet green peas, all bound together with a light creamy sauce.

SERVES 4   **PREPARATION TIME** 15 minutes   **COOKING TIME** 25 minutes

500 g (1 lb 2 oz) dried fettuccine or 600 g (1 lb 5 oz) fresh fettuccine (see pages 8–13)
155 g (5½ oz) asparagus spears
155 g (5½ oz/1 cup) fresh (or frozen) broad (fava) beans
30 g (1 oz) butter
1 celery stalk, sliced
155 g (5½ oz/1 cup) shelled fresh peas
310 ml (10¾ fl oz/1¼ cups) thin (pouring) cream
50 g (1¾ oz/½ cup) finely grated parmesan cheese

1 Cook the pasta in a large saucepan of boiling salted water, following the packet instructions, until al dente. Drain and return to the pan.

2 Meanwhile, cut the asparagus into small pieces. Bring a saucepan of water to the boil, add the asparagus and cook for 2 minutes. Use a slotted spoon to remove the asparagus from the pan and plunge into a bowl of iced water.

3 Cook the beans in a saucepan of boiling water for 1 minute. Use a slotted spoon to remove and transfer to cold water. Drain, then peel and discard the tough outside skin. (If you're using very young, fresh beans, the skins can be left on, but mature and frozen beans should be peeled.) Return the beans to the pan and cook for 2–5 minutes or until tender.

4 Heat the butter in a heavy-based frying pan over medium–low heat. Add the celery and stir for 2 minutes. Add peas and cream and cook gently for 3 minutes. Add the asparagus, broad beans and cheese and season with salt and freshly ground black pepper. Bring the sauce to the boil and cook for 1 minute. Add the sauce to the cooked pasta and toss well to combine.

TIP To get 155 g (5½ oz/1 cup) shelled fresh peas, you will need about 450 g (1 lb) of peas in the pod.

Tagliatelle with green olives and eggplant

This is a great option when you feel like a light pasta without a heavy, creamy sauce or a tomato-based one. The lemon juice brings this dish together, its tartness offsetting the salty olives and buttery eggplant. Swap the parsley for finely shredded celery leaves or mint if you like.

SERVES 4   **PREPARATION TIME** 10 minutes   **COOKING TIME** 10 minutes

500 g (1 lb 2 oz) dried tagliatelle or
   or 600 g (1 lb 5 oz) fresh tagliatelle
   (see pages 8–13)
175 g (6 oz/1 cup) green olives
1 large eggplant (aubergine)
2 tablespoons olive oil
2 garlic cloves, crushed
125 ml (4 fl oz/½ cup) lemon juice
2 tablespoons finely chopped
   flat-leaf (Italian) parsley
50 g (1¾ oz/½ cup) finely grated
   parmesan cheese

1 Cook the pasta in a large saucepan of boiling salted water, following the packet instructions, until al dente. Drain and return to the pan.

2 Meanwhile, chop the olives, removing the pits, and cut the eggplant into small cubes.

3 Heat the oil in a heavy-based frying pan over medium heat. Add the garlic and stir for 30 seconds. Add the eggplant and cook, stirring frequently, for 6 minutes or until tender.

4 Add the olives and lemon juice and season with freshly ground black pepper. Add the sauce to the pasta and toss. Serve in bowls, sprinkled with the parsley and cheese.

TIPS If you prefer, the eggplant can be salted to draw out any bitter juices. Sprinkle the cut eggplant liberally with salt and leave to stand for 30 minutes. Rinse well before using.

You probably won't need to add salt as the olives are already quite salty.

Weekends

Chicken and vegetable soup with parsley pistou

This hearty soup is a complete meal in itself, loaded with vegetables, rice and pasta and sublime flavours that hail from the Mediterranean. If you don't have time to poach a chicken, use leftover chicken and homemade stock from the freezer or a good-quality ready-made one.

SERVES 8   **PREPARATION TIME** 30 minutes (+ 1 hour cooling)   **COOKING TIME** 1 hour 10 minutes

60 ml (2 fl oz/¼ cup) olive oil
2 brown onions, chopped
1 celery stalk, finely chopped
2 carrots, cut into 1 cm (½ inch) pieces
1 small fennel bulb, trimmed, chopped into 1 cm (½ inch) pieces
4 garlic cloves, chopped
3 sprigs each thyme, oregano and flat-leaf (Italian) parsley
75 g (2¾ oz/⅓ cup) arborio rice
100 g (3½ oz) dried orecchiette
100 g (3½ oz) baby spinach leaves
75 g (2¾ oz/½ cup) frozen peas
shaved parmesancheese, to serve

POACHED CHICKEN
1 x 1.8 kg (4 lb) chicken, rinsed and patted dry with paper towel, fat trimmed
1 carrot, chopped
1 brown onion, halved
1 celery stalk, chopped
6 flat-leaf (Italian) parsley stalks

PARSLEY PISTOU
4 garlic cloves, chopped
1 cup firmly packed flat-leaf (Italian) parsley leaves
80 ml (2½ fl oz/⅓ cup) extra virgin olive oil

1 To make the poached chicken, put the chicken, carrot, onion, celery and parsley stalks in a stockpot. Cover with cold water, bring slowly to the boil and simmer for 40 minutes, skimming any scum from the surface. Turn off the heat and cool the chicken in the stock for at least 1 hour. Remove the chicken, then strain and reserve the stock. Cool, then skim the fat from the surface. Remove the skin and bones from the chicken and shred the flesh into bite-sized pieces.

2 To make the parsley pistou, crush the garlic and parsley to a paste using a mortar and pestle. Season with salt and freshly ground black pepper and gradually incorporate oil (*pic 1*).

3 Meanwhile, heat the oil in a large saucepan over low heat, add the onion, celery, carrot and fennel, cover and cook for 15 minutes or until the vegetables are soft (*pic 2*). Add the garlic and herbs and stir for 2 minutes.

4 Add 3 litres (105 fl oz) of the reserved stock, the rice and pasta to the pan. Bring to the boil, then reduce the heat to low and simmer, covered, for 8 minutes.

5 Remove the herb sprigs from the soup (*pic 3*). Add 3 cups of shredded chicken, the spinach and peas and simmer, uncovered, for 5 minutes or until the rice and pasta are just cooked.

6 Ladle the soup into bowls, stir in a spoonful of the pistou and sprinkle with the cheese.

1

2

3

> **TIP** The parsley pistou can also be made in a small food processor.

Open lasagne with rocket and walnut pesto

This is a great dish for entertaining as all the elements can be made ahead of time and all you need to do is layer the lasagne just before serving. It's a great vegetarian dish (carnivores won't even notice there's no meat!) and is as delicious to eat as it looks.

SERVES 4 **PREPARATION TIME** 25 minutes **COOKING TIME** 25 minutes

375 g (13 oz) fresh lasagne sheets (see pages 8–10)
1 tablespoon olive oil
100 g (3½ oz/2 cups) baby spinach leaves
1 garlic clove, sliced
2 tablespoons lemon juice
200 g (7 oz/1⅔ cups) crumbled marinated goat's feta cheese
2 tablespoons finely grated parmesan cheese

WALNUT PESTO
100 g (3½ oz/1 cup) walnuts
2 garlic cloves
2 large handfuls baby rocket (arugula)
1 large handful basil leaves
1 large handful flat-leaf leaves (Italian) parsley
100 ml (3½ fl oz) extra virgin olive oil
80 ml (2½ fl oz/⅓ cup) walnut oil
50 g (1¾ oz/½ cup) finely grated pecorino cheese
100 g (3½ oz/1 cup) finely grated parmesan cheese

1 To make the pesto, preheat the oven to 180°C (350°F/Gas 4). Rinse the walnuts in cold water, shake dry, spread on a baking tray and bake for 5–8 minutes or until light golden.

2 Transfer the walnuts to a food processor and add the garlic, rocket, basil and parsley. Use the pulse button to process the mixture just until it resembles coarse breadcrumbs. With the motor running, add the oils in a thin stream, then add the pecorino and parmesan and process for 40 seconds. Transfer to a bowl, cover with plastic wrap and set aside until needed.

3 Cut the lasagne sheets into sixteen 8 cm (3¼ inch) squares. Cook a few squares at a time in a large saucepan of boiling salted water for 4 minutes or until al dente. Lay them on a clean cloth and cover to keep warm while the remaining squares cook.

4 Heat the oil in a large frying pan over medium heat, add the spinach and garlic and cook until just wilted. Stir in the lemon juice, cover and keep warm.

5 Spoon 1 tablespoon of the pesto onto warmed plates and spread out with the back of the spoon to the size of one of the pasta squares. Cover with a pasta square, then divide one-third of the spinach evenly among the plates, on top of the pasta. Sprinkle one-third of the goat's feta evenly among the plates, cover with another pasta square and spread with some of the pesto. Repeat layering, finishing with a layer of pesto. Sprinkle with the grated parmesan and serve immediately.

Fettuccine with mussels, saffron and garlic

It's important to time this dish well, as you are cooking the mussels and the pasta simultaneously and then bringing them together just before serving. So make sure everything else is ready — the table set, the wine poured — so that as soon as the pasta and sauce are done, you're good to go.

SERVES 4 **PREPARATION TIME** 20 minutes **COOKING TIME** 25 minutes

2 large vine-ripened tomatoes
1 pinch saffron threads
30 g (1 oz) butter
1 brown onion, finely chopped
1 celery stalk, finely chopped
2 garlic cloves, crushed
250 ml (9 fl oz/1 cup) white wine
1 kg (2 lb 4 oz) large black mussels,
    bearded and scrubbed
400 g (14 oz) dried fettuccine or
    500 g (1 lb 2 oz) fresh fettuccine
    (see pages 8–13)
125 ml (4 fl oz/½ cup) pouring
    (whipping) cream
¼ cup flat-leaf (Italian) parsley
    leaves, chopped

1 Score a cross in the base of each tomato. Soak the tomatoes in boiling water for 1–2 minutes, drain and plunge into cold water briefly. Peel back the skin from the cross. Halve, remove the seeds and chop the flesh.

2 Place the saffron in a small bowl. Add 1 tablespoon warm water and stand for 5 minutes (*pic 1*).

3 Melt the butter in a large saucepan over medium–high heat. Add the onion, celery and garlic and cook, stirring occasionally, for 5 minutes or until the vegetables are softened. Add the saffron mixture and wine. Bring to the boil, then reduce the heat to low and simmer, uncovered, for about 5 minutes or until reduced by half. Add the mussels (*pic 2*) and cook, covered, for 5 minutes or until the mussels have opened. Discard any mussels that do not open.

4 Meanwhile, cook the pasta in boiling salted water for 1 minute less than on the packet instructions (the final cooking will occur when tossing the pasta with the sauce). Drain, place in a serving bowl and keep warm.

5 Add the cream to the mussels as soon as they open, pouring it into the base of the pan so it combines with the liquid in the pan straight away (*pic 3*), and bring to a simmer. Add the tomato and toss to combine. Taste and adjust the seasoning, then sprinkle with the parsley and serve with the pasta.

1

2

3

Creamy prawns with fettuccine

The key to this dish is not to overcook the prawns as you want the flesh to be tender and juicy. We've presented them whole in the dish, which looks great when you're entertaining, but you can roughly chop the prawn meat if you prefer.

SERVES 4 **PREPARATION TIME** 15 minutes **COOKING TIME** 15 minutes

500 g (1 lb 2 oz) dried fettuccine or
   600 g (1 lb 5 oz) fresh fettuccine
   (see pages 8–13)
30 g (1 oz) butter
1 tablespoon olive oil
6 spring onions (scallions), sliced
1 garlic clove, crushed
500 g (1 lb 2 oz) raw prawns
   (shrimp), peeled and deveined,
   leaving the tails intact
250 ml (9 fl oz/1 cup) pouring
   (whipping) cream
2 tablespoons chopped flat-leaf
   (Italian) parsley, to serve

1 Cook the pasta in a large saucepan of boiling salted water, following the packet instructions, until al dente. Drain and return to the pan.

2 Heat the butter and oil in a frying pan over low heat, add the spring onion and garlic and stir for 1 minute. Add the prawns and cook for 2–3 minutes or until the flesh changes colour. Remove the prawns from the pan and set aside. Add the cream to the pan and bring to the boil. Reduce the heat and simmer until the sauce begins to thicken. Return the prawns to the pan, season with salt and freshly ground black pepper, and simmer for 1 minute.

3 Add the sauce to the pasta and toss gently. Serve sprinkled with the parsley.

TIP For a variation on this recipe, in step 1 add 1 sliced red capsicum (pepper) and 1 very thinly sliced leek. Use scallops instead of prawns or a mixture of both.

Lemon and vegetable pasta salad

This is a great dish to sneak in a lot of different vegetables into a meal. The sour cream adds a touch of indulgence, while the lemon juice and chervil keep it fresh and light. You can easily replace some of the vegetables with whatever else is in season, such as asparagus, sugar snap peas and broad (fava) beans in spring, or zucchini (courgette) and butter beans in summer.

SERVES 4   **PREPARATION TIME** 20 minutes   **COOKING TIME** 15 minutes

250 g (9 oz) dried farfalle
80 ml (2½ fl oz/⅓ cup) olive oil
250 g (9 oz) broccoli, cut into
　　small florets
125 g (4½ oz) snow peas
　　(mangetout), topped and tailed
150 g (5½ oz) yellow squash,
　　cut into quarters
2 tablespoons sour cream
1 tablespoon lemon juice
2 teaspoons finely grated
　　lemon zest
1 celery stalk, thinly sliced
1 tablespoon chopped chervil,
　　plus sprigs, to garnish

1　Cook the pasta in a large saucepan of boiling salted water, following the packet instructions, until al dente. Drain well, toss with 1 tablespoon of the oil and set aside to cool.

2　Combine the broccoli, snow peas and squash in a large bowl, cover with boiling water and leave for 2 minutes. Drain, plunge into iced water, drain again and pat dry with paper towel.

3　Put the sour cream, lemon juice and zest and the remaining oil in a screw-top jar and shake for 30 seconds or until combined. Season with salt and freshly ground black pepper.

4　Combine the cooled pasta, celery and drained vegetables in a large bowl and sprinkle with the chopped chervil. Pour over the dressing and toss to combine. Garnish with the chervil sprigs and serve at room temperature.

Chicken ravioli with mushroom sauce

SERVES 8 as a starter   **PREPARATION TIME** 40 minutes (+ 1 hour chilling)   **COOKING TIME** 25 minutes

250 g (9 oz) skinless chicken
  breast fillets, trimmed
2 spring onions (scallions),
  finely chopped
1 egg white
185 ml (6 fl oz/¾ cup) thin
  (pouring) cream
1 quantity fresh pasta dough,
  rolled out and trimmed into
  64 squares, measuring 6.5 cm
  (2½ inches) (see pages 8–14)
1 egg, lightly beaten
finely grated or shaved parmesan
  cheese, to serve (optional)

MUSHROOM SAUCE
40 g (1½ oz) butter
1 tablespoon olive oil
500 g (1 lb 2 oz) button mushrooms,
  cleaned, thinly sliced
80 ml (2½ fl oz/⅓ cup) brandy
500 ml (17 fl oz/2 cups)
  thin (pouring) cream
250 ml (9 fl oz/1 cup) good-quality
  chicken stock
2 tablespoons lemon juice
⅓ cup finely snipped chives

1   Coarsely chop the chicken and put in a food processor with the spring onion, then process until finely minced (ground) (*pic 1*). Add the egg white and process until smooth. Transfer the mixture to a medium bowl, cover with plastic wrap and refrigerate for 1 hour.

2   Use a wooden spoon to gradually stir the cream into the chicken mixture until evenly incorporated. Season well with salt and freshly ground black pepper. To prevent the pasta from drying out, work in batches, leaving the rest covered with a clean cloth until needed. Place 5–6 pasta squares on a work surface and place 2 teaspoons of mixture on the centre of each. Brush the edges of the pasta lightly with a little of the egg (*pic 2*), cover each with another square, then firmly press the edges together to enclose the filling. Repeat with the remaining pasta and filling. Use a round 7 cm (2¾ inch) cutter to cut the ravioli into discs (*pic 3*). Place on a tray lined with baking paper, with baking paper separating each layer. Cover with plastic wrap and refrigerate until needed.

3   To make the mushroom sauce, melt the butter and oil in a large frying pan over high heat until foaming. Add the mushrooms and cook, stirring often, for 3–4 minutes or until tender and browned. Stir in the brandy and cook for 30 seconds. Stir in the cream, stock, lemon juice and chives and bring to a simmer. Simmer for 2 minutes or until thickened slightly. Season with salt and pepper. Remove from the heat, cover and set aside.

4   Bring a large saucepan of salted water to the boil. Add one-third of the ravioli and simmer for 4–5 minutes or until the pasta is al dente, the filling is cooked and they rise to the surface. Use a slotted spoon to remove the ravioli from the water and drain, then place them in the sauce, stirring gently to coat. Cook the remaining ravioli in two more batches and place in the sauce, adding a little cooking water to the sauce if it has thickened too much on standing.

TIP To make a cheat's version of ravioli, you can use store-bought fresh lasagne sheets or, even easier, use won ton wrappers, both readily available in the refrigerated section of supermarkets.

Tagliatelle with veal, wine and cream

You'll be well rewarded if you use fresh pasta instead of dried in this dish, as the fresh version will soak up the delicious creamy sauce infinitely more. A good-quality dry white wine is the secret to the tasty sauce, so open up a nice bottle, add some of it to the sauce and drink the rest for dinner. You could also use marsala or a dry Spanish sherry instead of white wine.

SERVES 4   **PREPARATION TIME** 15 minutes   **COOKING TIME** 30 minutes

500 g (1 lb 2 oz) veal scaloppine
   or escalopes, cut into thin strips
plain (all-purpose) flour, seasoned,
   for dusting
60 g (2¼ oz) butter
1 onion, sliced
125 ml (4 fl oz/½ cup) dry white
   wine
60 ml (2 fl oz/¼ cup) beef or
   chicken stock
170 ml (5½ fl oz) thin
   (pouring) cream
500 g (1 lb 2 oz) dried tagliatelle
   or 600 g (1 lb 5 oz) fresh tagliatelle
   (see pages 8–13)
1 tablespoon finely grated parmesan
   cheese, plus extra, to serve
   (optional)
flat-leaf (Italian) parsley leaves,
   to garnish

1 Coat the veal with the seasoned flour. Melt the butter in a frying pan over medium–high heat. Add the veal, in batches, and fry quickly until browned. Remove with a slotted spoon and set aside.

2 Reduce to medium heat, add the onion to the pan and stir until soft and golden. Pour in the wine and cook until evaporated. Add the stock and cream and season with salt and freshly ground black pepper. Reduce the sauce by half, and add the veal towards the end.

3 Meanwhile, cook the pasta in a large saucepan of boiling salted water, following the packet instructions, until al dente. Drain and transfer to a warm serving dish.

4 Stir the cheese through the sauce. Pour the sauce over the pasta. Serve with extra cheese, if desired, and garnish with the parsley.

Blue cheese and broccoli with rigatoni

You can use your favourite blue cheese in this dish. We've chosen a mild creamy blue but opt for something stronger, such as gorgonzola or Stilton, if you like. You can also replace the flaked almonds with toasted pine nuts or chopped toasted walnuts.

SERVES 4 **PREPARATION TIME** 15 minutes **COOKING TIME** 15 minutes

500 g (1 lb 2 oz) dried rigatoni
500 g (1 lb 2 oz) broccoli
1 tablespoon vegetable oil
1 onion, sliced
125 ml (4 fl oz/½ cup) dry
   white wine
250 ml (9 fl oz/1 cup) thin
   (pouring) cream
½ teaspoon hot paprika
150 g (5½ oz) creamy mild blue
   cheese, chopped into small pieces
2 tablespoons flaked almonds,
   toasted

1 Cook the pasta in a large saucepan of boiling salted water, following the packet instructions, until al dente. Drain and return to the pan.

2 Cut the broccoli into florets and steam or microwave them for 2–3 minutes or until tender, then drain well.

3 Heat the oil in a large saucepan over medium heat and cook the onion until soft. Add the wine and cream and simmer for 4–5 minutes or until reduced and thickened slightly. Stir in the paprika and cheese and season with salt and freshly ground black pepper.

4 Add the broccoli and sauce to the pasta and gently toss over low heat until well mixed and heated through. Serve sprinkled with the almonds.

TIP To toast the flaked almonds, cook in a dry frying pan over medium heat, shaking the pan occasionally, for 1–2 minutes or until lightly golden.

Clams with angel hair pasta and fennel

Take care when cooking the garlic in this recipe — you are aiming for a light golden colour, as burnt garlic will taste bitter. This dish depends on good timing — the pasta partially cooks while you are cooking the clams, then the drained pasta is added to the clams to finish cooking.

SERVES 4 **PREPARATION TIME** 10 minutes (+ 3 hours purging if needed) **COOKING TIME** 15 minutes

1.2 kg (2 lb 10 oz) live baby clams
    (vongole)
1 fennel bulb
80 ml (2½ fl oz/⅓ cup) extra virgin
    olive oil
3 garlic cloves, thinly sliced
½ teaspoon fennel seeds
½ teaspoon dried chilli flakes
170 ml (5½ fl oz) dry white wine
finely grated zest and juice
    of 1 lemon
400 g (14 oz) dried angel hair pasta
¼ cup flat-leaf (Italian) parsley
    leaves, chopped

1 When buying clams from the fishmonger, ask if they have been purged (stored in aerated salt water to eliminate sand). If not, place the clams in a bowl and wash them under cold running water, then add 60 g (2¼ oz) salt to 2 litres (70 fl oz) water and stand for several hours in a cool place (*pic 1*). This recreates their natural environment and they will breathe and filter the water, releasing any sand from within their shells.

2 Remove the fennel fronds and finely chop to obtain 2 tablespoons. Set aside. Use a mandolin to finely shave the fennel bulb (*pic 2*).

3 Heat 3 tablespoons of the oil in a large saucepan with a tight-fitting lid over medium–low heat, add the shaved fennel and cook for 2–3 minutes or until softened. Add the garlic, fennel seeds and chilli flakes. Cook for 1–2 minutes, stirring occasionally, just until the garlic starts to colour. Add the wine and lemon zest, increase the heat to high and bring to the boil.

4 Add the clams and cover. Allow the clams to steam for 3–4 minutes, shaking the pan occasionally or until all the shells are open (*pic 3*). Remove the pan from the heat and quickly discard any clams that haven't opened.

5 Meanwhile, cook the pasta in a large saucepan of boiling salted water, for 1 minute less than the recommended time on the packet. Drain, add to the clams and toss to combine for 1 minute to allow the pasta to absorb most of the liquid and finish cooking.

6 Add the parsley and lemon juice. Taste for seasoning, adding salt if desired. Drizzle with the remaining oil, toss and serve sprinkled with the fennel fronds.

1

2

3

TIP Serve this dish with a bowl in which each person can dispose of their clam shells. Finger bowls and generous-sized napkins are a good idea, too.

Giant pasta shells with ricotta and rocket

These giant seashells are as elegant as they are fun. The shell is the perfect vessel for a delicious filling. We've used ricotta, marinated artichoke, sun-dried tomato and roasted capsicum but you could add some pitted olives, chopped pancetta or tinned tuna too.

SERVES 6   **PREPARATION TIME** 30 minutes   **COOKING TIME** 1 hour

40 dried conchiglioni

600 ml (21 fl oz) tomato basil passata (puréed tomatoes) or bottled pasta sauce

2 tablespoons oregano leaves, chopped

2 tablespoons basil leaves

FILLING

500 g (1 lb 2 oz) ricotta cheese

100 g (3½ oz/1 cup) finely grated parmesan cheese

150 g (5½ oz) rocket (arugula), finely shredded

1 egg, lightly beaten

185 g (6½ oz) marinated artichokes, finely chopped

80 g (2¾ oz) sun-dried (sun-blushed) tomatoes, finely chopped

95 g (3¼ oz) roasted capsicum (pepper), finely chopped

CHEESE SAUCE

60 g (2¼ oz) butter

35 g (1¼ oz/¼ cup) plain (all-purpose) flour

750 ml (26 fl oz/3 cups) milk

100 g (3½ oz) gruyère cheese, grated

2 tablespoons chopped basil

1 Cook the pasta in a large saucepan of boiling salted water, following the packet instructions, until al dente. Drain and arrange the pasta on two baking trays to prevent them sticking together. Cover lightly with plastic wrap.

2 To make the filling, combine all the ingredients in a large bowl. Spoon the filling into the pasta shells, taking care not to overfill them or they will split.

3 To make the cheese sauce, melt the butter in a small saucepan over low heat. Add the flour and stir for 1 minute or until golden and smooth. Remove from the heat and gradually stir in the milk. Return to the heat and stir constantly until the sauce boils and begins to thicken. Simmer for a further minute. Remove from the heat and stir in the cheese with the basil and season with salt and freshly ground black pepper.

4 Preheat the oven to 180°C (350°F/ Gas 4). Spread 250 ml (9 fl oz/1 cup) of the cheese sauce over the base of a 3 litre (104 fl oz) capacity ovenproof dish. Arrange the pasta shells over the sauce, top with the remaining cheese sauce and bake for 30 minutes, or until the sauce is golden.

5 Pour the passata in a saucepan and add the oregano. Cook over medium heat for 5 minutes or until heated through. To serve, divide the sauce among warmed serving plates, top with the pasta shells and sprinkle with the basil.

Spaghetti with olives and capers

The crispy breadcrumbs add a wonderful crunch to this dish. If your olives or capers are very salty, you might like to freshen up the pasta with a handful of roughly chopped herbs, added to the sauce just before serving — basil, oregano, marjoram or parsley will do the trick.

SERVES 4 **PREPARATION TIME** 20 minutes **COOKING TIME** 20 minutes

170 ml (5½ fl oz) extra virgin olive oil

125 g (4½ oz/1½ cups) fresh white breadcrumbs

3 garlic cloves, finely chopped

45 g (1½ oz) tin anchovies (optional), drained and finely chopped

300 g (10½ oz) black olives, pitted and roughly chopped

6 roma (plum) tomatoes, peeled and chopped

2 tablespoons baby capers, rinsed

500 g (1 lb 2 oz) dried spaghetti or 600 g (1 lb 5 oz) fresh spaghetti (see pages 8–13)

1 Heat 2 tablespoons of the oil in a frying pan over medium heat. Add the breadcrumbs and cook, stirring continuously, until golden brown and crisp. Remove from the pan and set aside to cool completely.

2 Heat the remaining oil in the pan. Add the garlic, anchovies, if using, and olives and cook over medium heat for 30 seconds. Add the tomato and capers and cook for 3 minutes or until the tomato is soft.

3 Meanwhile, cook the pasta in a large saucepan of boiling salted water, following the packet instructions, until al dente. Drain and return to the pan. Add the tomato mixture and breadcrumbs and toss to combine.

TIP You probably won't need to add salt as the anchovies, olives and capers are already quite salty.

Fettuccine with asparagus, artichokes and creamy pesto sauce

Try to find artichoke hearts preserved in oil — they have a milder, less acidic flavour than those preserved in vinegar. Use homemade pesto if you can or buy it from a deli rather than a supermarket.

SERVES 4   **PREPARATION TIME** 10 minutes   **COOKING TIME** 25 minutes

2 bunches asparagus, trimmed
    and halved
250 g (9 oz) green beans, trimmed
350 g (12 oz) small marinated
    artichoke hearts, drained well
    and halved
500 g (1 lb 2 oz) dried fettuccine
    or 600 g (1 lb 5 oz) fresh
    fettuccine (see pages 8–13)
250 ml (9 fl oz/1 cup) pouring
    (whipping) cream
85 g (3 oz/¹⁄₃ cup) pesto
    (see page 33)
40 g (1¹⁄₂ oz/¹⁄₂ cup) shaved
    parmesan cheese, or to taste

1   Bring a saucepan of salted water to the boil, then cook the asparagus for 2 minutes or until bright green and just tender. Remove using a slotted spoon (*pic 1*) and cool under cold running water. Drain well. Cook the beans in the boiling water for 3 minutes or until just tender, then drain well and cool under cold running water (*pic 2*). Combine the cooked vegetables with the artichokes in a bowl and set aside.

2   Cook the pasta in a large saucepan of boiling salted water, following the packet instructions, until al dente. Drain well.

3   Bring the cream to the boil over medium heat in a large saucepan or large, deep frying pan. Simmer for 3 minutes or until reduced slightly, then stir in the pesto (*pic 3*). Add the pasta and vegetables, season with salt and freshly ground black pepper and toss to combine well. Cook, tossing often, over medium heat for 2–3 minutes or until the vegetables are heated through and the sauce has thickened slightly.

4   Divide among bowls, scatter over the cheese and serve.

1

2

3

TIP To trim asparagus, gently bend the spear. It will break at the natural division between the woody base and the tender upperpart of the stem.

Penne with pumpkin and cinnamon sauce

Not all pasta sauces need to be laden with tomatoes and this pumpkin, cinnamon and honey number is proof. This tasty combination is as comforting as it is delicious and the ideal meal when the weather is starting to get a little bit cooler.

SERVES 4   **PREPARATION TIME** 15 minutes   **COOKING TIME** 25 minutes

500 g (1 lb 2 oz) dried penne
25 g (1 oz) butter
1 onion, finely chopped
2 garlic cloves, crushed
1 teaspoon ground cinnamon
250 ml (9 fl oz/1 cup) pouring (whipping) cream
340 g (11¾ oz) pumpkin (winter squash), peeled, seeded and diced
1 tablespoon honey
35 g (1¼ oz/⅓ cup) finely grated parmesan cheese, plus extra, to serve
snipped chives, to garnish

1   Cook the pasta in a large saucepan of boiling salted water, following the packet instructions, until al dente. Drain and return to the pan.

2   Meanwhile, melt the butter in a frying pan over medium heat and cook the onion until soft and golden. Add the garlic and cinnamon and cook for another minute.

3   Pour the cream into the pan, add the pumpkin and honey and simmer for 5 minutes or until the pumpkin is tender, the sauce has reduced and has thickened slightly and is heated through.

4   Add the cheese and stir until it has melted. Season with salt and freshly ground black pepper. Pour the sauce over the pasta and toss until well combined. Serve sprinkled with the chives and extra cheese.

Pork and fennel tortellini with tomato sauce

SERVES 4   **PREPARATION TIME** 1 hour   **COOKING TIME** 25 minutes

400 g (14 oz) good-quality pork
   and fennel sausages
1 tablespoon olive oil
1 brown onion, chopped
2 garlic cloves, crushed
500 ml (17 fl oz/2 cups) tomato
   passata (puréed tomatoes)
pinch of white sugar
1 quantity fresh pasta dough
   (see page 8)
1 egg, lightly beaten
finely grated parmesan cheese,
   to serve

1   Remove and discard the sausage casings (*pic 1*) and refrigerate the meat until ready to use.

2   Heat the oil in a medium saucepan over medium heat. Cook the onion and garlic, stirring, for 5 minutes or until softened. Stir in the passata and 375 ml (13 fl oz/1½ cups) water. Simmer, covered, for 15 minutes. Season with the sugar, salt and freshly ground black pepper.

3   To prevent the dough from drying out, work in batches, using one-quarter of the dough at a time, leaving the rest covered with a clean cloth until needed. Roll out the pasta dough, following the step-by-step instructions on pages 10–11, to form sheets of pasta less than 1 mm (1/32 inch) thick and about 14 cm (5½ inches) wide (see page 15 for step-by-step photos of making tortellini). Work with one sheet at a time, leaving the others covered by a clean cloth. Cut out 6.5 cm (2½ inch) rounds, trying to minimise wastage as much as possible (*pic 2*).

4   Place about ¼ teaspoon of sausage meat into the centre of each round and brush the edges lightly with the egg. Fold into a half moon shape, pressing the edges to seal and taking care to expel any air. Wrap the two edges of the folded side around your fingertip (*pic 3*), brushing one edge lightly with the egg, and pinch to seal. Place, so that they are not touching, on trays lined with lightly floured baking paper. Repeat with the remaining dough and filling.

5   Cook the pasta in a large saucepan of boiling salted water until al dente. Break open one of the tortellini to check that the meat filling is cooked. If not, continue cooking for a little longer.

6   Reheat the sauce over medium heat. Drain the tortellini and add to the sauce. Stir over low heat until well coated. Serve sprinkled with the cheese and pepper.

1

2

3

Brandy chicken fettuccine

The secret to getting the mushrooms in this dish caramelised and crispy is slow cooking over low heat. It's also important not to overcrowd the pan, so if you don't have a large enough frying pan, cook the mushrooms in two or three batches.

SERVES 4 **PREPARATION TIME** 20 minutes **COOKING TIME** 20 minutes

10 g (¼ oz) dried porcini mushrooms
2 tablespoons olive oil
2 garlic cloves, crushed
200 g (7 oz) button mushrooms, sliced
125 g (4½ oz) prosciutto slices, chopped
500 g (1 lb 2 oz) dried fettuccine or 600 g (1 lb 5 oz) fresh fettuccine (see pages 8–13)
60 ml (2 fl oz/¼ cup) brandy
250 ml (9 fl oz/1 cup) thin (pouring) cream
1 barbecued chicken, shredded
155 g (5½ oz/1 cup) frozen peas
20 g (¾ oz/⅓ cup) finely chopped flat-leaf (Italian) parsley

1 Put the porcini mushrooms in a bowl and cover with boiling water. Set aside for 10 minutes, then drain, squeeze dry and roughly chop.

2 Heat the oil in a large, heavy-based frying pan over low heat. Add the garlic and cook, stirring, for 1 minute. Add the button and porcini mushrooms, along with the prosciutto, and cook, stirring often, for 5 minutes.

3 Meanwhile, cook the pasta in a large saucepan of boiling salted water, following the packet instructions, until al dente. Drain and return to the pan.

4 Add the brandy and cream to the mushroom mixture. Cook, stirring, over low heat for 2 minutes. Add the chicken, peas and parsley. Cook, stirring, for 4–5 minutes or until heated through. Add the chicken mixture to the hot pasta and mix until well combined.

TIP Chop the slices of prosciutto separately, otherwise they will stick together. Use bacon instead, if preferred. If porcini mushrooms are not available, use 30 g (1 oz) dried Chinese mushrooms.

Chicken pizzaiola

Pizzaiola means 'pizza style'. Most of the cooking for this dish is done in the oven, so you can largely set it and forget it until it's time to shred the chicken and cook the pasta.

SERVES 4 **PREPARATION TIME** 20 minutes **COOKING TIME** 1 hour 50 minutes

1 x 1.6 kg (3 lb 8 oz) chicken
2 tablespoons olive oil
1 large brown onion, thinly sliced
4 basil leaves
2 garlic cloves, crushed
1 tablespoon baby capers, rinsed and drained
4 anchovies, chopped
2 x 400 g (14 oz) tins chopped tomatoes
250 ml (9 fl oz/1 cup) chicken stock
60 g (2¼ oz/½ cup) pitted green olives, chopped
400 g (14 oz) dried pappardelle or 600 g (1 lb 5 oz) fresh pappardelle (see pages 8–13)
basil leaves and dried chilli flakes, to serve

1 Preheat the oven to 180°C (350°F/ Gas 4). Remove any excess fat from the chicken, then rinse in cold water and pat dry with paper towel (*pic 1*).

2 Heat the oil in a large flameproof casserole dish over medium heat. Add the onion and basil and cook, stirring occasionally, for 5 minutes or until the onion is softened. Add the garlic, capers and anchovies. Cook, stirring, for 1 minute or until the anchovies have dissolved. Add the tomatoes and stock (*pic 2*) and stir to combine. Add the chicken and bring to the boil. Partially cover with the lid, transfer to the oven and cook for 1½ hours.

3 Remove the chicken from the casserole. Place the casserole on the stovetop over medium heat and bring the cooking juices to the boil, then cook, stirring occasionally, for 10–15 minutes or until reduced.

4 When cool enough to handle, shred the chicken meat and discard the skin and bones. Return the chicken meat to the pan with the olives (*pic 3*). Cook, stirring, until heated through, then season with freshly ground black pepper.

5 Meanwhile, cook the pasta in a large saucepan of boiling salted water, following the packet instructions, until al dente. Drain well.

6 Divide the pasta among warmed plates, top with the sauce and scatter over the basil and chilli flakes to serve.

1

2

3

TIP You probably won't need to add salt as the anchovies and olives are already quite salty.

Chicken agnolotti with cream sauce

Agnolotti are half-moon shaped ravioli (they're sometimes referred to as mezzelune too). Adults and children alike will find these tempting. These are fun to make and a great way to get kids involved in cooking dinner. They are also an ideal parcel to hide vegetables from fussy eaters.

SERVES 4 as a starter   **PREPARATION TIME** 45 minutes   **COOKING TIME** 25 minutes

½ quantity fresh pasta dough,
    rolled out and 8 cm (3¼ inch)
    rounds cut out (see pages 8–14)
1 egg, lightly beaten
chives, to garnish (optional)

CHICKEN AND HAM FILLING
250 g (9 oz) skinless chicken breast
    fillets, trimmed and roughly
    chopped
1 egg, lightly beaten
pinch of ground white pepper
90 g (3¼ oz) ham or prosciutto
2 teaspoons finely snipped chives
2 teaspoons chopped marjoram

CREAM SAUCE
30 g (1 oz) butter
2 spring onions (scallions),
    finely chopped
2 tablespoons white wine
375 ml (13 fl oz/1½ cups) pouring
    (whipping) cream

1   To make the chicken and ham filling, chop the chicken in a food processor. Add the egg, pepper and ½ teaspoon of salt and process until finely chopped. Transfer to a bowl. Finely chop the ham or prosciutto and stir into the chicken with the herbs.

2   To prevent the pasta from drying out, work in batches, leaving the rest covered with a clean cloth until needed. Lay the pasta rounds on a work surface, six at a time, and put a teaspoonful of filling in the centre of each. Brush the edges with some of the egg, fold in half to form a half-moon shape and press the edges together firmly to seal. Place on a clean cloth and repeat with the remaining pasta rounds and filling.

3   To make the cream sauce, heat the butter in a large frying pan over medium–low heat, add the spring onion and cook for 2–3 minutes. Add the wine and cream and simmer until reduced. Season with salt and freshly ground black pepper.

4   Cook the agnolotti in batches in a large saucepan of boiling salted water for 3–4 minutes or until the pasta is al dente, the filling cooked and they float to the surface. Drain and serve with the sauce spooned over. Garnish with chives, if you like.

TIP To make a cheat's version of agnolotti, you can use store-bought fresh lasagne sheets or, even easier, use 250 g (9 oz) packet gow gee wrappers, both readily available in the refrigerated section of supermarkets.

Vegetable lasagne

You don't have to be a vegetarian to love this version of lasagne. The vegetable layers can be varied, depending on what is available. Use slices of sweet potato instead of pumpkin, a layer of sautéed mushrooms rather than spinach and leeks, or add pesto to the tomato sauce in place of fresh basil.

SERVES 8 **PREPARATION TIME** 1 hour 15 minutes (+ 10 minutes standing) **COOKING TIME** 1 hour 15 minutes

750 g (1 lb 10 oz) eggplant
(aubergine), cut into 1 cm
(½ inch) thick slices
125 ml (4 fl oz/½ cup) extra virgin
olive oil
4 x 400 g (14 oz) tins chopped
tomatoes
8 garlic cloves, chopped
1 teaspoon caster (superfine) sugar
⅓ cup basil leaves, torn
2 bunches English spinach, trimmed
and washed
1 large leek, white part only, chopped
20 g (¾ oz) butter
600 g (1 lb 5 oz) fresh lasagne sheets
(see pages 8–11)
500 g (1 lb 2 oz) pumpkin (winter
squash), peeled (peeled weight
415 g/14¾ oz), cut into 5 mm
(¼ inch) thick slices
100 g (3½ oz/¾ cup) finely grated
parmesan cheese

CHEESE SAUCE
90 g (3¼ oz) butter, chopped
90 g (3¼ oz) plain (all-purpose)
flour
750 ml (26 fl oz/3 cups) warm milk
75 g (2¾ oz/¾ cup, loosely packed)
coarsely grated cheddar cheese

1 Preheat oven to 200°C (400°F/Gas 6). Place eggplant on a baking tray and brush with 2 tablespoons oil. Season. Roast for 30 minutes, turning once, or until lightly browned (*pic 1*). Drain on paper towel.

2 Meanwhile, to make cheese sauce, melt butter in a medium saucepan over low heat, add flour and stir until dry and grainy. Gradually whisk in milk and bring to a simmer. Season. Simmer over low heat for 5 minutes, whisking occasionally or until thick. Remove from heat and stir in cheese. Cover with plastic wrap; cool slightly.

3 Meanwhile, in a large saucepan over medium heat, add tomatoes, 2 tablespoons oil, garlic and sugar and simmer for 8–10 minutes or until thick. Season and stir in basil.

4 Toss spinach in a large frying pan over medium heat for 2–3 minutes or until wilted. Drain. When cool, squeeze out moisture; chop. Heat remaining oil over low heat in a saucepan and cook until soft. Remove from heat, stir in spinach (*pic 2*). Season. Reduce oven to 180°C (350°F/Gas 4).

5 Rub butter over sides and base of a 3 litre (105 fl oz) casserole dish (about 19 x 35 x 7.5 cm/7½ x 14 x 3 inches) and place a layer of pasta over the base. Top with eggplant, then half the tomato sauce. Top with one-third of the cheese sauce (*pic 3*), then a layer of pasta, a layer of pumpkin, another third of the cheese sauce and another layer of pasta. Top with spinach mixture, remaining tomato sauce and another layer of pasta. Spread remaining cheese sauce on top and sprinkle with parmesan. Bake for 45 minutes or until browned and bubbling. Remove from oven and stand for 10 minutes before serving.

1

2

3

TIP The lasagne can be made a couple of hours ahead of time, refrigerated, then baked straight from the fridge. It might need up to 10 minutes more cooking time.

Grilled carbonara

A stylist's tip to present long pasta is to twirl the pasta into individual nests and place it in the dish prior to grilling. To make the nests, twirl the cooked ribbons of pasta many times around a long fork or a pair of tongs. This eliminates the inevitable tangled mass of pasta when you serve.

SERVES 4   **PREPARATION TIME** 10 minutes   **COOKING TIME** 15 minutes

250 g (9 oz) dried linguine

4 eggs

185 ml (6 fl oz/¾ cup) thin (pouring) cream

6 thin prosciutto slices, chopped

75 g (2½ oz/¾ cup) finely grated parmesan cheese

2 tablespoons snipped chives, plus extra, to garnish

30 g (1 oz) butter

1   Brush a shallow ovenproof dish with melted butter or oil. Preheat the grill (broiler) to moderately hot.

2   Cook the pasta in a large saucepan of boiling salted water, following the packet instructions, until al dente. Drain and return to the pan.

3   Meanwhile, whisk the eggs and cream together in a bowl, stir in the prosciutto, ½ cup of the cheese and the chives, and season with freshly ground black pepper.

4   Add the egg mixture and butter to the hot pasta and stir continuously over low heat for 1 minute or until the egg mixture begins to thicken slightly. Take care not to overcook the mixture, or you will end up with scrambled eggs. The mixture should be creamy and moist.

5   Pour the pasta into the dish and sprinkle with the remaining cheese. Place under the grill for a few minutes, until just set and lightly browned on top. Garnish with the chives.

Herb pappardelle with veal ragù

This dish is so easy — it's a great choice for a dinner party as you can make the ragù ahead of time, then the only thing you have to think about is cooking the pasta. The result is rustic but rewarding.

SERVES 6   **PREPARATION TIME** 15 minutes (+ 20 minutes soaking)   **COOKING TIME** 2 hours 15 minutes

5 g (⅛ oz) dried porcini mushrooms
4 veal shanks (about 1.1 kg/2 lb 7 oz)
1 tablespoon plain (all-purpose) flour
2½ tablespoons olive oil
2 brown onions, chopped
3 garlic cloves, finely chopped
1 tablespoon finely chopped rosemary
250 ml (9 fl oz/1 cup) red wine
500 ml (17 fl oz/2 cups) beef stock
400 g (14 oz) tin chopped tomatoes
60 g (2¼ oz/¼ cup) tomato paste (concentrated purée)
600 g (1 lb 5 oz) fresh herb pappardelle (see pages 8–13)
¼ cup flat-leaf (Italian) parsley, chopped

1   Preheat the oven to 200°C (400°F/Gas 6). Cover the porcini with 80 ml (2½ fl oz/⅓ cup) boiling water and set aside for 20 minutes. Strain, reserving the soaking liquid and discard any gritty residue.

2   Meanwhile, season the veal shanks with salt and freshly ground black pepper, then dust with flour (*pic 1*).

3   Heat the oil in a large flameproof casserole dish over medium heat. Brown the shanks on each side for 2–3 minutes or until golden brown all over (*pic 2*). Remove and set aside.

4   Reduce the heat to low, add the onion and cook, stirring often, for 3 minutes or until softened. Add the garlic and rosemary and cook, stirring, for 2 minutes or until light golden. Add half the wine to the casserole, increase the heat to medium and bring to the boil, scraping the base of the dish to dislodge any caramelised bits (*pic 3*).

5   Add the remaining wine, the stock, tomatoes, tomato paste, porcini and their soaking liquid and stir to combine. Return the shanks and any juices to the casserole. Bring to a simmer, cover and cook in the oven for 1 hour.

6   Remove the casserole from the oven and turn the shanks. Return to the oven for 1 hour or until the meat is falling from the bones. Remove the shanks from the liquid, place on a chopping board and use two forks to shred the meat into chunks (discarding any fat and sinew). Remove any marrow from the bones and reserve.

7   Return the meat and marrow to the casserole and place over low heat, season with salt and pepper and stir through half the parsley.

8   Meanwhile, cook the pasta in a large saucepan of boiling salted water, until al dente. Drain and place in a warmed serving bowl. Serve with the ragù, sprinkled with the remaining parsley.

1

2

3

TIP You might need to order veal shanks specially from your butcher.

Fettuccine with smoked salmon

Simple yet elegant, this would be ideal for a Sunday lunch or when entertaining friends. Just make sure you don't cook the smoked salmon — all you need to do is leave it in the hot pan with the sauce and the residual heat will warm it through.

SERVES 4 **PREPARATION TIME** 10 minutes **COOKING TIME** 10 minutes

100 g (3½ oz) smoked salmon
35 g (1¼ oz/¼ cup) sun-dried (sun-blushed) tomatoes
1 tablespoon olive oil
1 garlic clove, crushed
250 ml (9 fl oz/1 cup) thin (pouring) cream
¼ teaspoon mustard powder
15 g (½ oz/¼ cup) snipped chives, plus extra, to garnish
2 teaspoons lemon juice
500 g (1 lb 2 oz) dried fettuccine or 600 g (1 lb 5 oz) fresh fettuccine (see pages 8–13)
2 tablespoons finely grated parmesan cheese, to serve (optional)

1 Cut the smoked salmon into bite-sized pieces and the sun-dried tomatoes into long, thin strips. Set aside.

2 Cook the pasta in a large saucepan of boiling salted water, following the packet instructions, until al dente. Drain well and return to the pan.

3 Meanwhile, heat the oil in a frying pan over low heat, add the garlic and stir for 30 seconds. Add the cream, mustard powder and chives and season with salt and freshly ground black pepper. Bring to the boil, then reduce the heat and simmer, stirring, until the sauce begins to thicken. Add the salmon and lemon juice and stir to combine, then remove from the heat.

4 Toss the sauce through the pasta. Serve immediately, topped with the sun-dried tomato, extra chives and cheese, if desired.

Spaghettini with sardines, fennel and tomato

This is a classic Sicilian pasta dish, although we've simplified the method slightly. If you have difficulty finding fresh sardines, you could replace them with red mullet.

SERVES 4   **PREPARATION TIME** 15 minutes   **COOKING TIME** 35 minutes

3 roma (plum) tomatoes
100 ml (3½ fl oz) olive oil
3 garlic cloves, crushed
60 g (2¼ oz/1 cup) fresh rustic or
    sourdough breadcrumbs
1 red onion, thinly sliced
1 fennel bulb, quartered and
    thinly sliced
40 g (1½ oz) raisins
40 g (1½ oz/¼ cup) pine nuts,
    toasted
3–4 anchovies, chopped
125 ml (4 fl oz/½ cup) white wine
1 tablespoon tomato paste
    (concentrated purée)
350 g (12 oz) butterflied sardine
    fillets
⅓ cup flat-leaf (Italian) parsley
    leaves
500 g (1 lb 2 oz) dried spaghettini

1   Score a cross in the base of each tomato. Soak the tomatoes in boiling water for 1–2 minutes, drain and plunge into cold water briefly. Peel back the skin from the cross. Halve, remove the seeds and chop the flesh.

2   Heat 1 tablespoon of the oil and one-third of the garlic in a large frying pan over medium heat. Add the breadcrumbs and cook, stirring, until lightly golden (*pic 1*). Transfer to a plate.

3   Heat 60 ml (2 fl oz/¼ cup) of the oil in the same pan over medium–low heat and cook the onion, fennel and remaining garlic for 8 minutes or until soft. Add the raisins, pine nuts, anchovies and tomato (*pic 2*) and cook for a further 3 minutes. Stir in the wine, tomato paste and 125 ml (4 fl oz/½ cup) water. Simmer for 10 minutes or until the mixture thickens slightly. Set aside.

4   Pat the sardines dry with paper towel (*pic 3*) and heat the remaining oil in a frying pan over medium heat. Cook the sardines in batches for 1 minute or until cooked through. Take care not to overcook or they will break up. Set aside.

5   Cook the pasta in a large saucepan of boiling salted water, following the packet instructions, until al dente. Drain and return to the pan. Stir the sauce through the pasta. Add the sardines and parsley and half the breadcrumbs and toss gently. Sprinkle over the remaining breadcrumbs to serve.

TIPS   To toast the pine nuts, cook in a dry frying pan over medium heat, shaking the pan occasionally, for 1–2 minutes or until lightly golden.
Ask your fishmonger to butterfly the sardines for you.

Chicken ravioli with fresh tomato sauce

Make a double batch of both the sauce and ravioli and freeze the extra batches for another meal. The sauce will pair with any type of pasta or you can spread over a pizza base, and you can use the ravioli as soup dumplings or serve generously drizzled with pesto (see page 33).

SERVES 4   **PREPARATION TIME** 45 minutes   **COOKING TIME** 35 minutes

1 tablespoon olive oil
1 large onion, chopped
2 garlic cloves, crushed
90 g (3¼ oz/⅓ cup) tomato paste
   (concentrated purée)
60 ml (2 fl oz/¼ cup) red wine
170 ml (5½ fl oz) chicken stock
2 very ripe tomatoes, chopped
1 tablespoon chopped basil
finely grated parmesan cheese,
   to serve

RAVIOLI
200 g (7 oz) minced (ground)
   chicken
1 tablespoon chopped basil
25 g (1 oz/¼ cup) finely grated
   parmesan cheese
3 spring onions (scallions),
   finely chopped
50 g (1¾ oz) ricotta cheese
½ quantity fresh pasta dough,
   (see page 8)
1 egg, lightly beaten

1   Heat the oil in a saucepan over medium heat, add the onion and garlic and cook for 2–3 minutes, then stir in the tomato paste, wine, stock and tomato. Simmer over low heat for 20 minutes. Stir in the basil and season with salt and freshly ground black pepper.

2   Meanwhile, to make the ravioli filling, combine the chicken, basil, parmesan, spring onion and ricotta and season with salt and pepper.

3   To prevent the pasta dough from drying out, work in batches, using one-quarter of the dough at a time, leaving the rest covered with a clean cloth until needed. Roll out the pasta dough, following the step-by-step instructions on pages 10–11, to form sheets of pasta about 1 mm (¹⁄₃₂ inch) thick and about 14 cm (5½ inches) wide. Working with one sheet at a time, place slightly heaped teaspoons of the filling on one of the pasta sheets, leaving about 4 cm (1½ inches) in between each mound (see page 14). Brush around the filling with some egg. Place another pasta sheet on top, then press around the edge of each mound of filling to enclose it, taking care to expel any air.

4   Cut the ravioli into 6.5 cm (2½ inch) squares using a large knife or fluted pastry wheel if you have one. Place, so that they don't touch each other, on trays lined with lightly floured baking paper. Repeat with the remaining dough and filling.

5   Cook the pasta in a large saucepan of boiling salted water for 7 minutes or until al dente. Drain and divide among warmed plates. Serve with the tomato sauce spooned over and scatter over the cheese.

> **TIP** To make a cheat's version of ravioli, you can use store-bought fresh lasagne sheets or, even easier, use 250 g (9 oz) packet won ton wrappers, both readily available in the refrigerated section of supermarkets.

Orecchiette with Italian sausage and tomato

Italian sausages are typically rather coarsely textured and often robustly flavoured, for example with pork and fennel. If you can't find Italian sausage, substitute any well-flavoured one.

SERVES 4   **PREPARATION TIME** 15 minutes   **COOKING TIME** 30 minutes

6 ripe tomatoes
400 g (14 oz) Italian sausages
2 tablespoons olive oil
2–3 garlic cloves, crushed
1 red onion, thinly sliced
80 ml (2½ fl oz/⅓ cup) white wine
 or water
2 tablespoons tomato paste
 (concentrated purée)
½ teaspoon dried oregano
⅓ cup basil leaves, shredded, plus
 whole leaves, to garnish
500 g (1 lb 2 oz) dried orecchiette
grated pecorino cheese, to serve

1   Score a cross in the base of each tomato. Soak the tomatoes in boiling water for 1–2 minutes, drain and plunge into cold water briefly. Peel back the skin from the cross. Halve, remove the seeds and chop the flesh.

2   Remove the skin casings from the sausages and coarsely crumble the meat into bite-sized pieces.

3   Heat 1 tablespoon of the oil in a large frying pan over medium–low heat. Add the sausage and cook, turning occasionally, for 5 minutes. Remove with a slotted spoon and drain on paper towel (*pic 1*).

4   Add the remaining oil to the pan over medium heat. Cook the garlic and onion for 3 minutes, without letting them burn, then add the tomato, wine, tomato paste, oregano and shredded basil. Simmer for 20 minutes or until slightly thick (*pic 2*). Season with salt and freshly ground black pepper.

5   Meanwhile, cook the pasta in a large saucepan of boiling salted water, following the packet instructions, until al dente. Drain and return to the pan.

6   Return the sausage to the sauce (*pic 3*) and heat through for 2 minutes.

7   Toss the sauce through the pasta, garnish with the basil leaves and scatter over the cheese.

1

2

3

TIP You could also use conchiglie pasta for this dish.

Spaghetti with chicken meatballs

These meatballs will taste even better if you buy chicken thigh fillets from a butcher and ask them to mince it fresh for you instead of buying pre-minced meat. Or you could ground the chicken yourself using the pulse action of a food processor — just make sure to keep it coarse — or hand-chop the meat. Make sure you use the chicken on the day it's minced too.

SERVES 4　**PREPARATION TIME** 30 minutes (+ 30 minutes chilling)　**COOKING TIME** 1 hour 30 minutes

500 g (1 lb 2 oz) minced (ground) chicken

60 g (2¼ oz) finely grated parmesan cheese, plus extra, to garnish

160 g (5¾ oz/2 cups) fresh white breadcrumbs

2 garlic cloves, crushed

1 egg

1 tablespoon chopped flat-leaf (Italian) parsley

1 tablespoon chopped sage

60 ml (2 fl oz/¼ cup) vegetable oil

500 g (1 lb 2 oz) dried spaghetti or 600 g (1 lb 5 oz) fresh spaghetti (see pages 8–13)

2 tablespoons chopped oregano, to serve

TOMATO SAUCE

1 tablespoon olive oil

1 onion, finely chopped

2 kg (4 lb 8 oz) very ripe tomatoes, chopped

2 bay leaves

30 g (1 oz/1 cup, loosely packed) basil leaves

1 teaspoon coarsely ground black pepper

1　In a large bowl, combine the chicken, cheese, breadcrumbs, garlic, egg and herbs. Season with salt and freshly ground black pepper. Shape tablespoonsful of the mixture into balls and chill for about 30 minutes, to firm.

2　Heat the oil in a shallow frying pan over medium–high heat and cook the balls, in batches, until golden brown. Turn them often by gently shaking the pan. Drain on paper towel.

3　To make the tomato sauce, heat the oil in a large saucepan over medium–high heat, add the onion and fry for about 1–2 minutes or until softened. Add the tomato and bay leaves, cover and bring to the boil, stirring occasionally. Reduce the heat to low, partially cover and cook for 50–60 minutes.

4　Add the meatballs to the sauce, along with the basil and pepper and simmer, uncovered, for 10–15 minutes.

5　Meanwhile, cook the pasta in a large saucepan of boiling salted water, following the packet instructions, until al dente. Drain and return to the pan. Add some sauce to the pasta and toss to distribute. Serve the pasta topped with the remaining sauce and the meatballs, and sprinkled with the oregano and extra cheese, if desired.

Index

Published in 2013 by Murdoch Books Pty Limited.

Murdoch Books Australia
83 Alexander St
Crows Nest, NSW 2065
AUSTRALIA
Phone: +61 (0) 2 8425 0100
Fax: +61 (0) 2 9906 2218
www.murdochbooks.com.au
info@murdochbooks.com.au

For Corporate Orders & Custom Publishing contact
Noel Hammond, National Business Development Manager
Murdoch Books Australia

Publisher: Anneka Manning
Designers: Susanne Geppart and Robert Polmear
Photographers: Jared Fowler, Julie Renouf, George Seper
Stylists: Cherise Pegano (Koch), Marie-Helénè Clauzon
Food preparation for photography: Alan Wilson
Project Managers: Martina Vascotta and Belinda So
Editor: Melissa Penn
Production Manager: Karen Small
Recipe Development: Sonia Greig, Leanne Kitchen, Cathie Lonnie,
Anneka Manning, Lucy Nunes, Grace Campbell and the Murdoch
Books Test Kitchen
Home Economists: Grace Campbell, Dixie Elliot, Joanne Glynn,
Caroline Jones, Sharon Kennedy, Lucy Lewis, Sabine Spindler,
Allan Wilson
Production: Karen Small

Text and Design © Murdoch Books Pty Limited 2012

Photography © Louise Lister and Murdoch Books
Pty Limited 2012

A cataloguing-in-publication entry is available from the catalogue
of the National Library of Australia at www.nla.gov.au.

A catalogue record for this book is available from the British Library.

Printed by 1010 Printing International Limited, China

The Publisher and stylist would like to thank Breville
(www.breville.com.au) for lending equipment for use
and photography.

IMPORTANT: Those who might be at risk from the effects
of salmonella poisoning (the elderly, pregnant women, young
children and those suffering from immune deficiency diseases)
should consult their doctor with any concerns about eating
raw eggs.

OVEN GUIDE: You may find cooking times vary depending
on the oven you are using. For fan-forced ovens, as a general rule,
set the oven temperature to 20°C (35°F) lower than indicated in
the recipe.

MEASURES GUIDE: We have used 20 ml (4 teaspoon) tablespoon
measures. If you are using a 15 ml (3 teaspoon) tablespoon add an
extra teaspoon of the ingredient for each tablespoon specified.